0 meters   1000

0 yards   1000

EYEWITNESS TRAVEL

ROME

POCKET
GUIDE

LONDON, NEW YORK,
MELBOURNE, MUNICH AND DELHI
www.dk.com

ART EDITOR Priyanka Thakur

EDITOR Alka Thakur

DESIGNERS Rajnish Kashyap, Shruti Singhi

PICTURE RESEARCHER Taiyaba Khatoon

CARTOGRAPHY Kunal Singh

Conceived by Redback Publishing, 25 Longhope Drive, Farnham,
Surrey, GU10 4SN

Reproduced by Colourscan (Singapore)

Printed and bound in China by Leo Paper Products Ltd.

First published in Great Britain in 2006
by Dorling Kindersley Limited
80 Strand, London WC2R 0RL

11 12 13 14 10 9 8 7 6 5 4 3 2

Reprinted with revisions 2008, 2010

Copyright 2006, 2010 © Dorling Kindersley Limited, London
A Penguin Company

ISBN: 978-1-40535-321-2

The information in this
DK Eyewitness Travel Guide is checked regularly.

Every effort has been made to ensure that this book is as up-to-date as
possible at the time of going to press. Some details, however, such as
telephone numbers, opening hours, prices, gallery hanging
arrangements and travel information, are liable to change. The
publishers cannot accept responsibility for any consequences arising
from the use of this book, nor for any material on third-party websites,
and cannot guarantee that any website address in this book will be a
suitable source of travel information. We value the views and
suggestions of our readers highly. Please write to:
Publisher, DK Eyewitness Travel Guides,
Dorling Kindersley, 80 Strand, London WC2R 0RL.

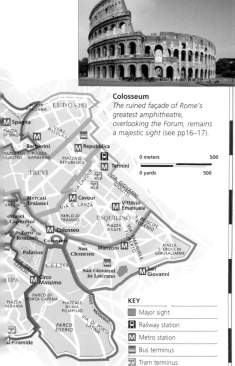

Colosseum

The ruined façade of Rome's greatest amphitheatre, overlooking the Forum, remains a majestic sight (see pp16–17).

0 meters		500
0 yards		500

KEY

■	Major sight
▤	Railway station
Ⓜ	Metro station
▤	Bus terminus
▤	Tram terminus

Discovery and Triumph of the Cross

Attributed to Antoniazzo Romano, this painting adorns Santa Croce in Gerusalemme (see p56).

Rome's Highlights

A vibrant modern capital, Rome derives its unique character from its ancient monuments, art treasures and timeless architecture in chuches, galleries and protected monuments. Here are some of the sights that have always dazzled and inspired visitors.

Museums and Galleries

Cortile Ottagonale at the Belvedere Palace, Vatican Museums

Galleria Nazionale d'Arte Antica
This state art collection is now divided between Palazzo Barberini *(see p82)* and Palazzo Corsini *(see p72)*. Both house paintings by masters such as Holbein.

Musei Capitolini
The papal art collections in this glorious museum are smaller than those found in the Vatican, but they are just as priceless *(see p10)*.

Museo e Galleria Borghese
This impressive collection of art comprises 15th–18th-century paintings, sculptures, bas-reliefs and mosaics *(see p86)*.

Museo Nazionale Romano
Archaeological finds and antiquities are carefully housed in four separate locations: the Baths of Diocletian, Palazzo Massimo *(see p49)*, Palazzo Altemps *(see p35)* and Crypta Balbi.

Vatican Museums
These galleries include the Graeco-Roman antiquities, the Etruscan Museum, four Raphael Rooms, the Collection of Modern Religious Art, the Sistine Chapel and the Picture Gallery *(see p78)*.

Squares and Fountains

Campo de' Fiori
A riot of colour during the morning market, this "field of flowers" is also a centre of Roman nightlife *(see p44)*.

Fontana delle Tartarughe
Giacomo della Porta designed this delightful fountain between 1581 and 1584 *(see p44)*.

Piazza del Popolo
Giuseppe Valadier's design for the former site of festivals and public executions has marble lions and fountains *(see p40)*.

Piazza Navona
This pedestrian paradise is filled with cafés and splashing fountains, such as Bernini's Fontana dei Quattro Fiumi *(see p32)*.

Trevi Fountain
Throwing coins into this 1732 Nicola Salvi fountain is believed to ensure a return to Rome *(see p48)*.

Detail of Fontana dei Quattro Fiumi

The striking dome of St Peter's, designed by Michelangelo

Churches and Basilicas

San Clemente
This unpretentious yet compelling church provides a concise Roman history lesson in one concentrated location *(see p56)*.

Santa Maria del Popolo
Legend has it that Nero was buried here. In 1099, in a vision, the Virgin told Pope Paschal II to dig up the evil emperor's bones and build a chapel *(see p40)*. The church has two great paintings by Caravaggio and frescoes by Pinturicchio.

Santa Maria Maggiore
One of Rome's greatest basilicas, this 5th-century church is full of Byzantine splendour *(see p52)*.

Santa Maria sopra Minerva
Rome's only Florentine Gothic church, built around 1280, houses Michelangelo's *Christ the Redeemer (see pp26–7)*.

St Peter's Basilica
The basilica's cavernous interior, a giant jewel-box of colour, is best appreciated when all the lights are on *(see pp76–7)*. The magnificent dome was designed by none other than Michelangelo.

Ancient Sites

Colosseum
The world's greatest amphitheatre has been the archetype for the popular sports stadiums *(see pp16–17)*. When Emperor Titus inaugurated it in AD 80, he declared 100 days of celebratory games.

Trajan's Column
Commemorating the emperor's victories over the Dacians *(see p18)*. The reliefs on the column realistically chronicle scenes from the two campaigns in AD 101–102 and AD 105–106.

A view of the Pantheon

Forum
An apparent shambles of ruins and weeds today, the Forum was the symbol of civic pride for 1,000 years. Its many attractions include the Curia, the Temple of Vesta and the House of Vestal Virgins *(see pp14–15)*.

Palatine Hill
The birthplace of Rome and later the home of its leaders' opulent homes, it now serves as a bucolic setting for a romantic stroll *(see pp20–23)*.

Pantheon
Hadrian built this striking structure, after the 1st-century BC temple burned down *(see pp28–9)*.

CAPITOL

The hub of religious and political life of ancient Romans, the Capitol proclaimed Rome's authority as *caput mundi*, head of the world. It has remained the seat of municipal government throughout the city's history, and is now home to some of its most spectacular sights.

SIGHTS AT A GLANCE

Churches and Temples
Capitoline Temple of
  Jupiter **5**
San Marco The Evangelist
  at the Capitol **7**
Santa Maria in Aracoeli **4**

Museums and Galleries
Capitoline Museums: Palazzo
  dei Conservatori **2**

Capitoline Museums:
  Palazzo Nuovo **1**
Palazzo Venezia
  and Museum **6**

Historic Streets and Piazzas
Piazza del Campidoglio **3**

SEE ALSO

• *Street Life p11*

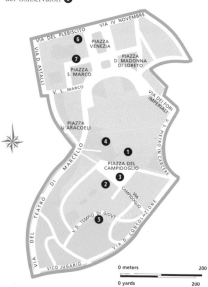

◀ Statue of Marcus Aurelius on Michelangelo's Piazza del Campidoglio

Dying Gaul *in Palazzo Nuovo*

Capitoline Museums: Palazzo Nuovo ❶

Map E4. Musei Capitolini, Piazza del Campidoglio 1. Closed Mon, 1 Jan, 1 May, 25 Dec. Adm charge is valid for Palazzo dei Conservatori.

Inaugurated in 1471 by Pope Sixtus IV, Palazzo Nuovo was designed by Michelangelo. It was the world's first public museum, mainly containing restored ancient sculpture, including the famed Capitoline Venus as well as Roman copies of Greek masterpieces such as the soulful *Dying Galatian* from the 3rd century BC.

Capitoline Museums: Palazzo dei Conservatori ❷

Adm charge for Palazzo Nuovo is valid for Palazzo dei Conservatori.

The seat of the city's magistrates during the late Middle Ages, this palazzo

A relief displayed in the courtyard of the Capitoline Museums

houses original 16th- and 17th-century art and Classical statues. An entire floor is dedicated to paintings by Veronese, Tintoretto, Rubens and Caravaggio. Meetings are occasionally held in the frescoed halls of the museum.

Piazza del Campidoglio ❸

Map E4.

In 1546, Michelangelo drew up plans for renovating the Capitol. Completed in the 17th century, the piazza retained some of the original design, including the double flight of steps for Palazzo Senatorio and placement of ancient sculptures. At the centre stands a replica of a statue of Marcus Aurelius.

Ceiling commemorating Battle of Lepanto in Santa Maria in Aracoeli

Santa Maria in Aracoeli ❹

Map E4. Scala dell'Arce Capitolina 14. Open daily. Free.

The 6th-century church stands on the site of the ancient temple of Juno Moneta. Its 22 columns come from ancient structures. The most famous feature is a tiny statue with reputedly miraculous powers, the *Santo Bambino*, a 15th-century figure of the Child Christ.

Capitoline Temple of Jupiter ❺

Map E4. Via del Tempio di Giove.
Adm charge.

The major temple in ancient
Rome was founded around
509 BC on the southern
summit of the Capitoline Hill.
Traces remain of the Greek
structure of the temple, as
well as the Roman podium
which mostly lies beneath the
Museo Nuovo wing of the
Palazzo dei Conservatori.

Palazzo Venezia and Museum ❻

Map E4. Via del Plebiscito 118.
Closed Mon, 1 Jan, 25 Dec. Adm
charge.

The 15th-century Palazzo was
built by Pope Paul II. Passing
into Austrian hands in 1797,
the palazzo was retrieved by
the state in 1916. Mussolini
used it as his headquarters.
The museum here houses
Renaissance art, Baroque
sculptures and 15th- to
18th-century Italian art.

San Marco The Evangelist at the Capitol ❼

Map E4. Piazza San Marco 48.
Open daily. Free.

The relics of its founder, Pope
Mark, lie under the altar of
this 4th-century church. It was
embellished by a succession
of popes, with magnificent
apse mosaics, ceilings and
colonnades. The aisles feature
funerary monuments.

San Marco's apse mosaic of Christ,
with Gregory IV on the far left

STREET LIFE

RESTAURANTS

Ichnos
Map E4. Via delle Botteghe
Oscure 33. Tel 06 686 5673.
Expensive
*A Sardinian-themed
restaurant offering
Mediterranean cooking, with
an emphasis on seafood.*

Vecchia Roma
Map E5. Piazza Campitelli 18.
Tel 06 686 4604.
Expensive
*Romantic restaurant with
frescoed interiors and creative
Roman cuisine. In one of the
city's most evocative squares.*

See p96 for price codes.

CAFÉS

Caffè Capitolino
Map E5 Piazzale Caffarelli 4.
*Little-known café in the Musei
Capitolini, with spectacular
views from the terrace.*

The Glass Bar & Restaurant
Map E4. Via di S.Eufemia 5.
*A modern, elegant bar
specializing in aperitifs,
cocktails and light lunches.*

SHOPPING

Limentani
Map E4. Via del Portico
d'Ottavia 47. *This store is
stocked with an extraordinary
array of household goods and
kitchenware.*

FORUM

The Forum was the centre of political, judicial and commercial life in ancient Rome. Beginning humbly almost 3,000 years ago, it rose in stature as Rome's power grew. Dominating the area is the imposing shell of the 1st century AD Colosseum, once the hub of entertainment.

SIGHTS AT A GLANCE

Churches and Temples
Temple of Antoninus
  and Faustina **7**
Temple of Saturn **4**
Temple of Vesta **5**

Historic Buildings
Basilica of Constantine
  and Maxentius **8**
Colosseum pp16–17 **9**
Curia **2**

House of the
  Vestal Virgins **6**
Mamertine Prison **14**
Trajan's Markets **11**

Arches and Columns
Arch of Constantine **16**
Arch of Septimius
  Severus **3**
Arch of Titus **10**
Trajan's Column **12**

Ancient Sites
Forum of Augustus **13**
Forum of Nerva **15**
Rostra **1**

SEE ALSO

• *Street Life p17.*

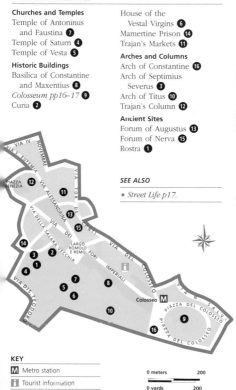

KEY

M Metro station

i Tourist information

| 0 meters | | 200 |
| 0 yards | | 200 |

◀ *The Forum, with the Colosseum rising behind Santa Francesca Romana*

A view of the ruins of the Imperial Rostra, once a prominent dais

Rostra ❶

Map F5. Entrances: Largo della Salaria Vecchia 5/6 and Via di S.Gregorio 30. Closed 1 Jan, 25 Dec. Tours of newly excavated sites available. Adm charge.

Decorated with iron-sheathed prows (*rostra*) of the ships captured at the Battle of Antinum in 338 BC, this renowned platform was used by politicians to address the crowd. Mark Antony's immortal "Friends, Romans, Countrymen" oration, after the assassination of Julius Caesar in 44 BC, is the one speech most remembered.

Curia ❷

Map F5. Open daily, except 1 Jan, 25 Dec. Adm charge.

Diocletian's Curia stands on the ruins of the Senate, which was built by Caesar at the edge of the Forum. A 1937 restoration of the Curia retains its original polychrome inlaid floor, its risers, where the 300 senators sat, and the speaker's platform. Inside, two relief panels show Trajan's good works.

The façade of the present-day Curia

Arch of Septimius Severus ❸

Map F5. Open daily, except 1 Jan, 25 Dec. Adm charge.

Dating from AD 203, this triumphal arch celebrates the emperor's Middle Eastern victories. Originally, the inscription along the top of the arch was to Septimius and his two sons, Caracalla and Geta, but later Caracalla murdered Geta, and had his brother's name removed. During the Middle Ages the central arch served as a barber's shop.

Ionic capitals on the surviving columns of the Temple of Saturn

Temple of Saturn ❹

Map F5. Open daily, except 1 Jan, 25 Dec. Adm charge.

A high platform, eight columns and a section of entablature constitute the remains of the temple. Originally built in 497 BC, the present structure dates from 42 BC. Saturn, the mythical god-king of Italy, presided over a Golden Age from which slavery, private property, crime and war were absent. Saturnalia, celebrated each December, was very similar to modern-day Christmas.

Temple of Vesta

Map F5. Open daily, except 1 Jan, 25 Dec. Adm charge.

The circular 2nd-century building, with elegant fluted columns, was the centre for one of the oldest cults in Rome. Six Vestal Virgins, chosen from noble families, kept alight the sacred flame of Vesta, the goddess of the hearth. The virgins enjoyed high status, and upon retirement were free to live the rest of their lives as ordinary citizens.

Temple of Vesta

Temple of Antoninus and Faustina

Map F5. Church open on Thu; ring the bell.

This excellently preserved temple was dedicated by Antonius Pius in AD 141 to his late wife Faustina. Converted into a church in the 11th century, the building has a Baroque façade oddly rising above the porch of the Roman temple. Note the griffins carved along the side frieze. The current church dates from 1601.

House of Vestal Virgins

Map F5. Open daily, except 1 Jan, 25 Dec. Adm charge.

The most evocative part of the Forum was originally a huge three-storey complex, with rooms arranged around a central courtyard. Overlooking ponds of water lilies and goldfish is a row of eroded statues of senior Vestals from the 3rd and 4th centuries AD. The better-preserved examples were transferred to the Museo Nazionale Romano *(see p49)*.

Basilica of Constantine and Maxentius

Map F5. Open daily, except 1 Jan, 25 Dec. Adm charge.

The basilica's three vast, coffered barrel vaults proclaim the Forum's largest structure, begun in AD 308 under Maxentius. The project was completed during the reign of Constantine, whose statue once adorned the apse. The building, like other Roman basilicas, was used as the legal and financial centre of the Empire.

A row of eroded statues lining the pond at the House of Vestal Virgins

Colosseum 🔾

Built in AD 72–80, Rome's greatest amphitheatre symbolized the imperial fetish for gory spectacle. Its practical design, with 80 arched entrances, allowed easy access to 50,000 spectators. The Colosseum's architectural splendour is still visible in its ruins.

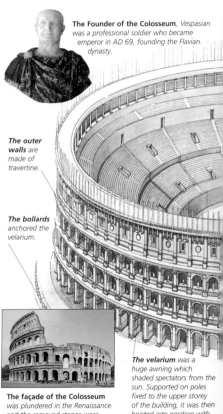

The Founder of the Colosseum, *Vespasian was a professional soldier who became emperor in AD 69, founding the Flavian dynasty.*

The outer walls *are made of travertine.*

The bollards *anchored the velarium.*

The façade of the Colosseum *was plundered in the Renaissance and the removed stones were used to build several palaces, bridges and parts of St Peter's.*

The velarium *was a huge awning which shaded spectators from the sun. Supported on poles fixed to the upper storey of the building, it was then hoisted into position with ropes anchored to bollards outside the stadium.*

Internal Corridors
were designed to allow the large and often unruly crowd to move freely and to be seated within 10 minutes of arriving at the Colosseum.

The vomitorium *was the exit used from each numbered section.*

Brick *formed the inner walls.*

The podium *was a large terrace where the emperor and the wealthy upper classes had their seats.*

Corinthian columns

Ionic columns

Doric columns

Entry routes *to take the spectators to their seats were reached by means of staircases to the various levels of the amphitheatre.*

Arched entrances, *80 in total, were all numbered to let in the vast crowds that attended the fights.*

VISITORS' CHECKLIST

Map F5. Piazza del Colosseo. Tel 06 3996 7700. Open 8:30am–1 hour before sunset daily. Closed 1 Jan, 25 Dec. Adm charge. Beware of unlicensed "gladiators" charging for photographs – negotiate a fee up front.

Dedication to Titus and Vespasian on the Arch of Titus

Arch of Titus 10

Map F5. Open daily, except 1 Jan, 25 Dec. Tours of newly excavated sites available. Adm charge.

This triumphal arch was erected in AD 81 by Emperor Domitian in honour of his brother, Titus, and his father, Vespasian, for quelling the Jewish Revolt. Reliefs show soldiers sacking Jerusalem's Holy of Holies and plundering sacred objects, including a golden menorah.

Trajan's Markets 11

Map F5. Mercati di Traiano, Via IV Novembre 94. Tel 06 679 0048. Open Tue–Sun, except 1 Jan, 1 May, 25 Dec.

One of the wonders of the Classical world, Emperor Trajan's visionary complex of 150 shops and offices was the ancient equivalent of the modern shopping centre. Today only a hint remains of this architectural gem by Apollodorus of Damascus,

The façade of the Trajan's Markets, as seen today

which once sold everything from luxury items imported from the Middle East to fresh local produce.

Trajan's Column 12

Map F5. Via dei Fori Imperiali. Open daily, except 1 Jan, 25 Dec. Adm charge.

Trajan inaugurated this elegant marble column in AD 113 to celebrate his victory in Dacia. The two campaigns against the Dacians are illustrated on the column, which is pierced with small windows to illuminate its internal spiral staircase. At its base, the ashes of Trajan and his wife were kept in a golden urn.

Podium of the Temple of Mars in the Forum of Augustus

Forum of Augustus 13

Map F5. Piazza del Grillo 1. Open by appt only. Adm charge.

The victory of Augustus over Julius Caesar's assassins, Brutus and Cassius, is celebrated in this forum, half of which is now hidden below Mussolini's Via dei Fori Imperiali. At its centre, the Temple of Mars is identified by its steps and four Corinthian columns. Originally, it had a statue of Mars, resembling Augustus, whose statue was placed against the Suburra wall.

Mamertine Prison ⑭

Map F5. Clivo Argentario 1.
Open daily. Donation expected.

Below the 16th-century church of St Joseph of the Carpenters is a dank dungeon in which, according to Christian legend, St Peter was imprisoned. He is said to have caused a spring to bubble up into the cell, and used the water to baptize his guards. The prison, also known as Tullianum, was in an old cistern with access to the city's main sewer. The lower cell was used for executions and bodies were thrown into the sewer.

Forum of Nerva ⑮

Map F4. Via dei Fori Imperiali (reached through Forum of Augustus). Tel 06 3996 7700. Open by appt only. Adm charge.

A long corridor with a colonnade along the sides and a Temple of Minerva at one end, the Forum of Nerva was begun by Domitian and completed in AD 97. Excavations have unearthed only a portion of the forum, which includes the base of the temple and two columns that formed part of the original colonnade.

North side of the Arch of Constantine, facing the Colosseum

Arch of Constantine ⑯

Map F5. Via di San Gregorio.
Free.

Erected in AD 315, this arch celebrated Constantine's victory over Maxentius. Most of the embellishments were scavenged from earlier monuments. There are statues of Dacian prisoners taken from Trajan's Forum and reliefs of Emperor Marcus Aurelius.

STREET LIFE

RESTAURANTS	BARS
Baires	**Al Vino Al Vino**
Map F4. Via Cavour 315. Tel 06 6920 2164.	**Map F4**. Via dei Serpenti 19. *Convivial and very well-stocked wine bar.*
Moderate	
Traditional Argentinian food, live tango music weekday evenings.	**Angelino ai Fori**
	Map F4. Largo C. Ricci 40. *Wonderful alfresco setting for a pre-dinner cocktail.*
Cavour 313	
Map F4. Via Cavour 313. Tel 06 678 5496.	**Oppio Caffé**
Cheap	**Map F5**. Via delle Terme di Tito 72. *A well-located, lively café with outdoor tables and an amazing view.*
Charming wood-panelled interior, tasty hot specials.	
See p96 for price codes.	

PALATINE

Archaeology supports the Palatine's mythical links with the founding of Rome by Romulus and Remus. With fragrant pines, this ancient site was also home to the great orator Cicero and the lyric poet Catullus. The area is dominated by the ruins of the Domus Augustana and the Domus Flavia.

SIGHTS AT A GLANCE

Temples
Temple of Cybele **5**

Historic Buildings
Domus Augustana **2**
Domus Flavia **1**
House of Livia **4**

Ancient Sites
Huts of Romulus **6**
Stadium **3**

Parks and Gardens
Farnese Gardens **7**

SEE ALSO

• *Street Life p23*

KEY

M Metro station

0 meters   200
0 yards   200

◀ *Towering ruins of the Palace of Septimius Severus on the Palatine hill*

Marble pavement in the courtyard of Domus Flavia

Domus Flavia ❶

Map F5. Via di San Gregorio 30. Closed 1 Jan, 25 Dec. Adm charge includes entry to the Palatine Museum and the Colosseum *(see pp16–17)*.

This imperial edifice was the official wing of a palace, built in AD 81 by Domitian. Once imposing in scale and design, the Domus Flavia today survives mainly as remains of the Basilica, where justice was dispensed; the Aulia Regia or throne room; and the Lararium, a shrine for the household gods.

Domus Augustana ❷

Same as Domus Flavia.

The Domus Augustana was the private wing of Domitian's palace. On the upper level a high brick wall remains, with some traces of its two courtyards. The far better-preserved lower level is closed to the public,

though its sunken courtyard, with the geometric foundations of a fountain, can be seen from above.

Stadium ❸

Same as Domus Flavia.

Part of Domitian's palace, the Stadium was possibly a public arena or a private track for exercising horses. The alcove in the eastern wall could have held a box from which the emperor watched races. In the 6th century, the Ostrogothic king, Theodoric, added the tiny oval enclosure at the southern end.

The 1st-century Stadium, as seen from the south

House of Livia ❹

Same as Domus Flavia. Closed to the public.

One of the best preserved on the Palatine, this 1st-century BC structure formed part of the residence of the Emperor Augustus and his wife, Livia. Unlike later Imperial palaces, it was a

Remains of the Domus Augustana and the Palace of Septimius Severus

modest home, reflecting the austere taste of Augustus. Though the rooms are small, there are several mosaic pavements and wall frescoes.

Temple of Cybele ❺

Same as Domus Flavia.

One of the oldest Oriental religions to come to Rome, in 191 BC, this orgiastic cult was centred around the Great Mother. The annual festival of Cybele, in early spring, culminated with ceremonial self-castration by the priests. Other than the decapitated statue of the goddess and a platform with a few column stumps and capitals, little remains of the temple.

Huts of Romulus ❻

Same as Domus Flavia.

According to legend, after killing his brother Remus, Romulus founded a village on the Palatine. In the 1940s a series of holes was found filled with earth lighter in colour than the surrounding soil. Archaeologists deduced that these holes originally held the supporting poles of three Iron Age huts – the first foundations of Rome.

Farnese Gardens ❼

Same as Domus Flavia.

In the 16th century Cardinal Alessandro Farnese asked Vignola to design a garden on the ruins of Tiberius's palace. The result was one of the first botanical gardens in Europe, introducing a number of plants to Italy and Europe, including *Acacia farnesiana*. Re-landscaped following the excavation of the Palatine, the gardens are still graceful, with tree-lined avenues and rose gardens.

A glorious view of the Farnese pavilions on the Palatine

PIAZZA DELLA ROTONDA

The historic Piazza della Rotonda has been at the centre of uninterrupted economic and political activity for nearly 2,000 years. At its heart, the Pantheon is a striking example of ancient European architecture. It is Rome's financial hub today, as well as the focus of its social life.

SIGHTS AT A GLANCE

Churches and Temples
Gesù **4**
Pantheon pp28–29 **6**
Sant'Ignazio di Loyola **2**
Santa Maria sopra
  Minerva **5**
Temple of Hadrian **1**

Historic Buildings
Palazzo Borghese **7**
Palazzo Doria Pamphilj **3**

Column
Column of Marcus
  Aurelius **8**

SEE ALSO

• *Street Life p27*

KEY

M Metro station

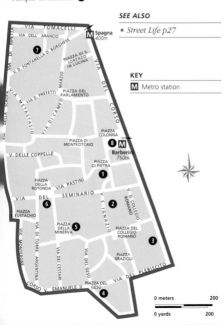

◄ *Piazza della Rotonda seen through the columns of the Pantheon*

Temple of Hadrian ❶

Map E4. La Borsa, Piazza di Pietra. Open for occasional exhibitions.

Deifying Emperor Hadrian, this temple was dedicated by his son, Antoninus Pius, in AD 145. The remains of the temple are visible in a building that today houses the Roman stock exchange. A number of relics, representing conquered Roman provinces, are now in the Palazzo dei Conservatori.

Sant'Ignazio di Loyola ❷

Map E4. Piazza di Sant'Ignazio. Open daily. Free.

Pope Gregory XV built this church in 1626 in honour of St Ignatius of Loyola, founder of the Society of Jesus. Its ornate interior creates a sense of theatre, while the Latin-cross plan features an apse and many side chapels. A cupola was planned but never built. In its place, a fake perspective was painted.

Illusionistic ceiling in the crossing of Sant'Ignazio di Loyola

Palazzo Doria Pamphilj ❸

Map E4. Via del Corso 305. Closed Thu, 1 Jan, Easter Sun, 1 May, 15 Aug, 1 Nov, 25 Dec. Adm charge.

The oldest parts of this great island of stone date from

1435. Later, it acquired new features such as courtyards and flanking wings. The Pamphilj family's collection of paintings from the 15th to 18th centuries is housed in the gallery here, including the famed portrait of Pope Innocent X by Velazquez.

Chapel of Sant'Ignazio, Gesù

Gesù ❹

Map E4. Piazza del Gesù. Open daily. Free.

Celebrated throughout the Catholic world, the 16th-century Gesù sits on the spot of the first Jesuit church to be built in Rome. Its Counter-Reformation Baroque architecture proclaims the church's two major functions: a large nave with side pulpits for preaching to great crowds, and a main altar as the centrepiece for the mass. The illusionistic decoration in the nave and dome was added a century later.

Santa Maria sopra Minerva ❺

Map E4. Piazza della Minerva 42. Open daily (occasionally closed Sun pm). **Cloister** Open Mon–Sat. Free.

Built on ancient ruins, this 12th-century church displays

an impressive range of Italian art. Prominent are the 13th-century tombs and priceless 15th-century Tuscan and Venetian art. The Roman Renaissance is represented in the tombs of Medici popes. The piazza in front has Bernini's famous statue of an elephant with an obelisk on its back.

Pantheon ⑥

See pp28–9

Palazzo Borghese ⑦

Map E3. Largo della Fontanella di Borghese 22. Closed to the public.

Pope Paul V hired Flaminio Ponzio to re-design the original, less elaborate building into a grand residence for his family. The additional features included a wing, a porticoed courtyard and a great *nymphaeum*, the Bath of Venus. For more than two centuries this palazzo

housed the Borghese family's collection of paintings, now in the Galleria Borghese.

Relief of the emperor's campaigns on the Column of Marcus Aurelius

Column of Marcus Aurelius ⑧

Map E3. Piazza Colonna. Free.

Erected after the death of Marcus Aurelius in AD 180, this column commemorated his victories over the barbarian tribes of the Danube. Though an imitation of the Column of Trajan (*see p18*), it is more akin to the Arch of Constantine (*see p19*) in its stress on the supernatural, as can be seen in the relief.

STREET LIFE

RESTAURANTS

Riccioli Café
Map D3. Via delle Coppelle 13.
Tel 06 6821 0313.
Expensive
The speciality at this youthful restaurant is fresh fish dishes and sushi.

La Campana
Map E3. Vicolo della Campana 18, Tel 06 686 7820.
Moderate
Historic trattoria, serving great tripe and chicken dishes since 1518. Mouthwatering desserts include cooked cherries with ice cream.

Maccheroni
Map D3. Piazza della Coppelle 44. Tel 06 6830 7895.
Moderate
Traditional Roman dishes. Alfresco dining in summer.

BARS AND CAFÉS

Cafe Sant'Eustachio
Map D4. Piazza Sant'Eustachio 82. *Reputedly serves the best cappuccino in town. The recipe is a well-guarded secret.*

Tartarughino
Map D3. Via della Scrofa 1.
Ideal for an elegant night out. A piano bar and a good wine list.

See p96 for price codes.

Pantheon ❻

This magnificent structure, with a domed interior, was built in AD 118–125 by Emperor Hadrian, who designed it to replace an earlier temple. The shrines lining the Pantheon's walls range from the Tomb of Raphael to those of the kings of modern Italy.

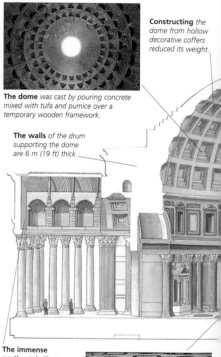

The dome was cast by pouring concrete mixed with tufa and pumice over a temporary wooden framework.

Constructing the dome from hollow decorative coffers reduced its weight.

The walls of the drum supporting the dome are 6 m (19 ft) thick.

The immense portico is built on the foundations of Agrippa's temple.

The marble floor, restored in 1873, preserves the original Roman design.

Brick arches *embedded in the structure of the wall act as internal buttresses, distributing the weight of the dome.*

Tomb of Raphael
The artist's body rests below a Madonna by Lorenzetto (1520).

Oculus

The portico *is enclosed by granite columns.*

VISITORS' CHECKLIST

Map D4. Piazza della Rotonda. Open 8.30am–7.30pm Mon–Sat, 9am–6pm Sun. Closed 1 Jan, 1 May, 25 Dec. Free.

PIAZZA NAVONA

The elongated oval of Rome's loveliest square hints that it is built atop Domitian's ancient stadium. Three exquisite fountains form a perfect setting for this lively pedestrian paradise. Baroque, the predominant style of the piazza, is visible in many of the area's churches.

SIGHTS AT A GLANCE

Churches and Temples
Chiesa Nuova ⑩
San Luigi dei Francesi ④
San Salvatore in Lauro ⑫
Sant'Andrea della Valle ⑥
Sant'Ivo alla Sapienza ⑤
Santa Maria della Pace ③

Museums
Museo Napoleonico ⑬

Historic Buildings
Palazzo Altemps ⑭
Palazzo Massimo alle Colonne ⑦

Fountains and Statues
Fontana dei Quattro Fiumi ①
Pasquino ⑧

Historic Streets and Piazzas
Piazza Navona ②
Via dei Coronari ⑪
Via del Governo Vecchio ⑨

SEE ALSO

• *Street Life p35*

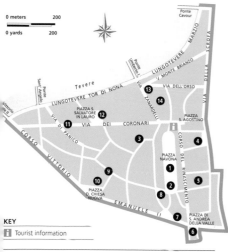

KEY

🛈 Tourist information

◀ *Piazza Navona, with the Fontana del Moro and Sant'Agnese in Agone*

Fontana dei Quattro Fiumi ❶

Map D4. Piazza Navona.

Bernini designed this magnificent fountain in 1651 for Pope Innocent X Pamphilj, whose coat of arms – the dove and the olive branch – decorates the pyramid rock formation supporting the Roman obelisk. The great rivers, Ganges, Danube, Nile and Plate, are represented by four giants. The Nile's veiled head symbolizes the river's unknown source, while the athletic figure of the River Plate, cringing with arm upraised, is supposed to express Bernini's fear that the church will collapse.

Symbolic figure of the River Ganges in the Fontana dei Quattro Fiumi

Piazza Navona ❷

Map D4.

Rome's most beautiful Baroque piazza stands on the ruins of the 1st-century Domitian's Stadium. The square's unique character was created by its three fountains, which date from the 16th and 17th centuries, but have been altered

Palazzo Pamphilj in Piazza Navona

several times since. Until the 19th century, the fountain outlets were stopped during August to flood the piazza for the rich to splash around in carriages. Today, it is lively in all seasons, with its numerous shops and cafés. Its largest building, the 17th-century frescoed Palazzo Pamphilj, is now the Brazilian embassy and cultural centre.

Santa Maria della Pace ❸

Map D3. Arco della Pace 5. Open Mon, Wed, Sat. Free.

Pope Sixtus IV della Rovere asked Baccio Pontelli to build this church following the end of the war with Turkey. In 1504, Bramante added a cloister, strictly following Classical rules of proportion. Pietro da Cortona added a charming semi-circular portico in 1656. The interior houses Raphael's famous frescoes of four *Sybils*, and four *Prophets* by his pupil Timoteo Viti. Baldassarre Peruzzi also did some work in the church, as did the architect Antonio da Sangallo the Younger.

San Luigi dei Francesi ❹

Map D3. Piazza di San Luigi dei Francesi 5. Closed Thu pm. Free.

A last resting place for many French luminaries, the French national church was completed in 1589, with contributions from Giacomo della Porta and Domenico Fontana. Three Caravaggios are dedicated to St Matthew in one of the chapels here. Painted between 1597 and 1602, these were the artist's first great religious works. All of them display a highly dramatic use of light and, even more strikingly, very disquieting realism.

Shield linking symbols of France and Rome on San Luigi's façade

Sant'Ivo alla Sapienza ❺

Map D4. Corso del Rinascimento 40. Open Sun morning only. Free.

Unlike any other Baroque church, this Borromini-designed one has a lantern crowned with a cross on top of a dramatic twisted spiral – a distinctive feature on Rome's skyline. Based on a ground design of great geometrical complexity, the walls beautifully combine concave and convex surfaces. The church stands in the small courtyard of the Palazzo della Sapienza, seat of the old University of Rome from the 15th century until 1935.

Sant'Andrea della Valle ❻

Map D4. Piazza Vidoni 6. Open daily. Free.

With a flamboyant Baroque façade, this church is the scene of the first act of Puccini's opera, *Tosca*. The gilded interior dazzles as light filters through high windows. The two Sienese popes, Pius II and Pius III, are buried here. The famed 17th-century dome, the largest in Rome after St Peter's, was built by Carlo Maderno and painted with splendid frescoes by Domenichino and Giovanni Lanfranco. The latter's lavish style can be seen in the dome fresco, *Glory of Paradise*. Domenichino painted the scenes from the life of St Andrew around the apse and altar. In the Strozzi Chapel, built in the style of Michelangelo, the altar has copies of the *Leah* and *Rachel* by Michelangelo in San Pietro in Vincoli.

Dome of Sant'Andrea della Valle

Roman column, Palazzo Massimo

Palazzo Massimo alle Colonne ❼

Map D4. Corso Vittorio Emanuele II 141. Chapel open 7am–1pm 16 Mar. Free.

Baldassare Peruzzi built this palazzo for the Massimo family, whose home, ravaged in 1527, had stood on the ruined Domitian Theatre. Peruzzi's originality is visible in the curved façade, the small square upper windows, the courtyard and the stuccoed vestibule. The family chapel is opened to the public once a year.

Pasquino ❽

Map D4. Piazza di Pasquino.

Once part of a Hellenistic group, this faceless, armless statue probably represents "Menelaus with the body of Patroclus". In 1501, it was placed near the shop of a cobbler, Pasquino, who scribbled satirical comments on it. The "talking statue" has stood in the same corner since, as an emblem of popular culture.

Pasquino, Rome's "talking statue"

Via del Governo Vecchio ❾

Map D4.

Named after the seat of papal government in the 17th and 18th centuries, the street is lined with 15th- and 16th-century houses and small workshops. Its main palazzo is also called Palazzo Nardini, from the name of its founder.

Chiesa Nuova ❿

Map D4. Piazza della Chiesa Nuova. Open daily.

The most appealing of the Counter Reformation saints, San Filippo Neri built this new church to replace its old medieval predecessor. After his death, Pietro da Cortona decorated the dome and apse, while Rubens painted three sanctuary canvases.

Via dei Coronari ⓫

Map D3.

This street is named after the rosary makers and sellers that used to line the way when it was on the main pilgrimage route to St Peter's. Now bustling with antiques dealers, the street still retains many of its original buildings from the 15th and 16th centuries.

San Salvatore in Lauro ⓬

Map D3. Piazza San Salvatore in Lauro 15. Open daily. Free.

The 16th-century church is named after the laurel grove that grew here in ancient times. The bell tower and sacristy were

18th-century additions by Nicola Salvi. A chapel houses Cortona's *The Birth of Jesus*, while the convent of San Giorgio has a lovely Renaissance cloister, a frescoed refectory and a monument to Pope Eugenius.

Museo Napoleonico

Map D3. Piazza di Ponte Umberto 1. Open Tue–Sun. Closed 1 Jan, 1 May, 25 Dec. Adm charge.

Assembled in 1927, this collection houses furnishings, *objets d'art* and memorabilia that belonged to the extensive Bonaparte clan, including an Indian shawl that Napoleon wore during his exile on St Helena.

Palazzo Altemps ⑭

Map D3. Piazza Sant'Apollinare 46. Open Tue–Sun. Adm charge.

Restored as a museum in the 1990s, this 15th-century palazzo boasts a fine group of Classical sculpture, such as *Dionysus with Satyr* and *Apollo Playing the Lute*. The Ludovisi Throne, a set of 5th-century reliefs, depicts a woman rising from the sea, believed to be Aphrodite.

Side relief of the Ludovisi Throne, Palazzo Altemps

STREET LIFE

RESTAURANTS

Lilli
Map D3. Via Tor di Nona 23.
Cheap
Ultra-traditional eatery.

Il Convivio
Map D3. Vicolo dei Soldati 31.
Expensive
Strictly seasonal cuisine. Ideal for a special night out.

BARS AND PUBS

Il Desiderio Preso Per La Coda
Map D3. Vicolo della Palomba 23. *Cool cocktail/wine bar.*

Caffè Chiostro
Map D3. Via della Pace. *Bar inside an art gallery.*

Caffè della Pace
Map D3. Via della Pace 3–7. *Still a place to see and be seen.*

Etablì
Map D3. Vicolo della Vacche 9/9a. *Ultra-stylish lounge bar mixing traditional with modern.*

SHOPPING

Ai Monasteri
Map D4. Corso Rinascimento 72. *Homemade goodies, from cosmetics to honey, by monasteries from across Italy.*

Calzoleria Petrocchi
Map D3. Via dell'Orso 25. *High-end shoe store, started by Tito Petrocchi, who once shod glamorous stars.*

L'Artigianato
Map D3. Piazza Navona 84. *Italian glass, marble and handmade gifts.*

See p96 for price codes.

PIAZZA DI SPAGNA

So named because it is home to the Spanish Embassy, the palm tree-lined Piazza di Spagna is one of the liveliest squares in the city. It was the haunt of English aristocrats and rich north Europeans in the 18th century, and still draws crowds of locals and tourists to its elegant shops.

SIGHTS AT A GLANCE

Churches
Santa Maria dei Miracoli and
 Santa Maria in
 Montesanto **8**
Santa Maria del
 Popolo **11**
Trinità dei Monti **5**

Museums and Galleries
Casa di Goethe **7**
Keats-Shelley
 Memorial House **3**

Historic Buildings
Villa Medici **6**

Arches, Gates and Columns
Porta del Popolo **12**

Historic Streets and Piazzas
Piazza del Popolo **10**
Piazza di Spagna **2**
Spanish Steps **4**
Via Condotti **1**

Monuments and Tombs
Ara Pacis **13**
Mausoleum of Augustus **14**

Parks and Gardens
Pincio Gardens **9**

SEE ALSO

• Street Life p41

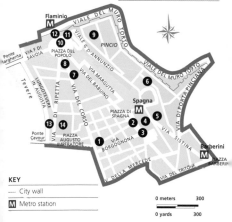

KEY
— City wall
Ⓜ Metro station

| 0 meters | 300 |
| 0 yards | 300 |

◀ *The Spanish Steps leading up to the church of Trinità dei Monti*

View along Via dei Condotti towards the Spanish Steps

Via dei Condotti ❶

Map E3.

Named after the conduits that carried water to the Baths of Agrippa near the Pantheon, Via dei Condotti is now home to shops owned by some of Rome's leading designers such as Gucci, Valentino, Prada and Armani. Stores selling shoes and other leather goods are also well represented. The street is extremely popular with tourists and locals for early evening strolls.

Piazza di Spagna ❷

Map E2.

The Piazza di Spagna has long been the haunt of foreign visitors and expatriates. In the 18th century Spain's ambassador to the Holy See had his headquarters on the square, and the area around it was deemed to be Spanish territory. In the 18th and 19th centuries, the square was full of hotels for aristocrats and

wealthy tourists, as well as artists, writers and composers. Even today, the hourglass-shaped piazza, surrounded by tall, shuttered houses painted in muted shades, is crowded with tourists and locals. The Fontana della Barcaccia, designed either by Bernini or his less famous father Pietro, is the least showy of Rome's Baroque fountains.

Keats-Shelley Memorial House ❸

Map E3. Piazza di Spagna 26. Open Mon–Sat. Closed 1 Jan, 25 Dec. Adm charge.

The pink-stuccoed apartment overlooking the Spanish Steps, where 25-year-old John Keats drew his last, consumptive breath, has been turned into a modest little museum dedicated to the Romantic-era British poets, such as Shelley and Byron, who lived part of their lives in Rome. Main displays include documents, letters, copies of publications, as well as Keats' death mask.

Shelley's bust by Moses Ezekiel

Spanish Steps ❹

Map E2. Scalinata della Trinità dei Monti, Piazza di Spagna.

One of the city's most dramatic and distinctive landmarks, the Spanish Steps were built by the French in 1725 to link the Trinità dei Monti church with the Piazza di Spagna. The Rococo design, featuring straight sections, curves and terraces, is attributed to Francesco de Sanctis, an Italian architect. When the Victorian novelist Charles Dickens visited Rome, he reported that the steps were the meeting place for artists' models, who would dress in colourful traditional costumes, hoping to catch the attention of a wealthy artist. These are now a popular place to sit, write postcards, take photos, busk or watch the passers-by.

Trinità dei Monti's bell towers

The Spanish Steps in spring with azaleas in full bloom

Trinità dei Monti ⑤

Map E2. Piazza della Trinità dei Monti. Open daily. Free.

With stunning views of Rome from its twin bell-towered façade, the Trinità dei Monti was founded by the French in 1495. Although it was later badly damaged, there are still traces of attractive late-Gothic latticework in the vaults of the transept. The interconnecting side chapels are decorated with Mannerist paintings, including two fine works by Daniele da Volterra, the artist who was

commissioned by Pope Pius IV to paint clothes on the nudes in Michelangelo's *Last Judgment*.

Villa Medici ⑥

Map E2. Accademia di Francia a Roma, Viale della Trinità dei Monti 1. Open for exhibitions and concerts. Adm charge.

Superbly positioned on the Pincio hill above Piazza di Spagna, this villa was bought by Cardinal Ferdinando de' Medici in 1576. It now houses the renowned French Academy, founded by Louis XIV in 1666. After the Academy moved to the Villa Medici in 1803, musicians were also admitted, prominently, Berlioz and Debussy.

Casa di Goethe ⑦

Map E2. Via del Corso 18. Open Tue–Sun. Adm charge.

The German poet, dramatist and novelist Johann Wolfgang von Goethe lived in this house from 1786 until 1788 and worked on a journal that eventually formed part of his travel book, *The Italian Journey*.

Traditional carnival band in the Piazza del Popolo

Santa Maria dei Miracoli and Santa Maria in Montesanto ⑧

Map D2. Piazza del Popolo. Open daily.

The two 17th-century churches prove the genius of Carlo Rainaldi in achieving symmetry despite space limitations. In order to create the illusion of similarity, Santa Maria dei Miracoli was given a circular dome and Santa Maria in Montesanto an oval one to squeeze it into the narrower site.

Pincio Gardens ⑨

Map E2. Il Pincio.

Giuseppe Valadier designed the beautiful 19th-century gardens, much cherished by

The Casina Valadier restaurant in the Pincio Gardens

Romantic writers. The main square boasts panoramic sunsets. Casina Valadier is a legendary café on the grounds. Other charms include the water clock, the busts of various notables and an Egyptian-style obelisk erected by Hadrian.

Piazza del Popolo ⑩

Map D2.

This former site of festivals and public executions was expanded into an elegant piazza by Valadier in 1811–23. Four Egyptian lion fountains were added at the base of one of Rome's oldest obelisks, a 1200 BC Ramases II monolith brought from Egypt by Augustus.

Santa Maria del Popolo ⑪

Map E2. Piazza del Popolo 12. Open daily.

One of Rome's greatest stores of artistic treasures, this early Renaissance church was commissioned by Pope Sixtus IV della Rovere in 1472. Among the artists who worked on the building were Andrea Bregno and Pinturicchio. Later additions were made by Bramante and Bernini.

Porta del Popolo

Map D2. Between Piazzale Flaminio and Piazza del Popolo.

This grand 16th-century gate was modelled on a Roman triumphal arch. A century later, Pope Alexander VII asked Bernini to decorate the inner face.

Agrippa, Mausoleum of Augustus

Ara Pacis ⑬

Map D2. Lungotevere in Augusta. Open Tue–Sun. Closed 1 Jan, 1 May, 25 Dec.

Built by Augustus Caesar during 13–9 BC, this "altar of peace" originally stood on the Corso, but its fantastic reliefs were excavated and reconstituted here by Mussolini. It is now housed in a striking building designed by Richard Meier.

Mausoleum of Augustus ⑭

Map D2. Piazza Augusto Imperatore. Currently closed for restoration. Tel 06 6710 3819.

A weedy ruin ringed with cypresses, this grand imperial tomb was once the most prestigious burial place in Rome. It was built by Augustus in 27 BC, his ashes later joined by those of Tiberius, Nerva, Marcus Agrippa and Marcellus.

STREET LIFE

RESTAURANTS

Edy
Map E2. Vicolo del Babuino 4.
Tel 06 3600 1738.
Cheap
Lovely seafood and Roman dishes. The candlelit tables out front are a nice touch.

Hassler-Roof Garden
Map E2. Piazza Trinità dei Monti 6. Tel 06 699 340.
Expensive
Opulent restaurant, offering delicious food and a bird's-eye view of the roofs of old Rome.

CAFÉS

Antico Caffè Greco
Map E3. Via dei Condotti 86.
Rome's premier literary café since 1760, popular with the 19th-century Romantic poets.

Babington's Tea Rooms
Map E2. Piazza di Spagna 23.
Exclusive spot for tea and other dainty British edibles.

SHOPPING

Bulgari
Map F3. Via dei Condotti 10.
Timeless store, selling glitzy jewellery. There's also an affordable range of watches.

E&R Danon
Map E2. Via Margutta 36–7.
Stocks mostly 18th- to early 20th-century Oriental carpets and prayer rugs.

Modigliani
Map E3. Via dei Condotti 24.
Tasteful home accessories, from gadgets to glassware.

See p96 for price codes.

CAMPO DE' FIORI

This fascinating part of Renaissance Rome is also a hub of shopping and nightlife, centered around the market square of Campo de' Fiori. Its open-air market preserves the lively, bohemian atmosphere of the medieval inns that once thrived here. The area also contains Palazzo Farnese and Palazzo Spada, where powerful Roman families built their fortress-like houses. The Portico of Octavia and the Theatre of Marcellus are examples of the city's many-layered history.

SIGHTS AT A GLANCE

Museums and Galleries
Palazzo Spada ②

Historic Buildings
Palazzo Farnese ③

Fountains
Fontana delle Tartarughe ④

Historic Streets and Piazzas
Campo de' Fiori ①
Ghetto and Synagogue ⑥

Ancient Sites
Theatre of Marcellus ⑤

SEE ALSO

• Street Life p45

◄ Giordano Bruno's statue overlooking fruit stalls in the Campo de' Fiori

Market stalls in Campo de' Fiori

Campo de' Fiori ❶

Map D4. Piazza Campo de' Fiori.

A backdrop for princes as well as pilgrims in the Middle Ages, the "Field of Flowers" today pulsates with a morning market and colourful nightlife. On the darker side, this lively area was also the centre of the Inquisition's executions. The statue of the hooded philosopher Giordano Bruno, who was martyred for heresy in 1600, overlooks all.

Palazzo Spada ❷

Map D5. Piazza Capo di Ferro 13. Galleria Spada open Tue–Sun. Closed 1 Jan, 25 Dec. Adm charge.

With an elegant stuccoed courtyard and relief-embellished façade, this majestic 1550 palace contains a 17th-century gallery, which is a clever study in illusory perspective. Designed by Borromini, on the orders of Cardinal Spada and his brother, Galleria Spada houses a wide collection, mainly featuring paintings by Rubens, Dürer and Guido Reni.

Palazzo Farnese ❸

Map D4. Piazza Farnese. Not open to the public.

A shining example of Renaissance style, this 16th-century palace was originally built for Cardinal Alessandro Farnese. It reflects the genius of Antonio da Sangallo as well as Michelangelo, who contributed to the great cornice and central window of the main façade, and the third level of the courtyard.

Majestic façade of Palazzo Farnese

Fontana delle Tartarughe ❹

Map E4. Piazza Mattei.

Giacomo della Porta designed this delightful 16th-century fountain to decorate the palace of the Mattei family. The four bronze youths were sculpted by Taddeo Landini. The tortoises (*tartarughe*) were added a century later, possibly by Bernini.

Fontana delle Tartarughe

Theatre of Marcellus ❺

Map E5. Via del Teatro di Marcello. Open daily. Free.

First built by Augustus in 23 BC and dedicated to Marcellus, his nephew and son-in-law, the theatre once held up to 20,000 people. Three beautiful Corinthian columns and a section of freize still stand close to the largely ruined structure.

Ghetto and Synagogue ❻

Map E5. Synagogue, Lungotevere dei Cenci. Open daily. Closed on Jewish public hols. Adm charge.

The Jews, who arrived in Rome as traders in the 2nd century BC, flourished during the Imperial age. In the 16th century, however, they were ordered by Pope

Paul IV to live inside a high-walled enclosure. Persecution started again in 1943, when many Jews were deported to German concentration camps. Many of them still live in the former Ghetto and the medieval streets retain much of their old character. The imposing 1904 Synagogue houses a Jewish museum which describes the history of the community through torahs and other artifacts.

Synagogue overlooking the Tiber

STREET LIFE

RESTAURANTS

Camponeschi
Map D4. Piazza Farnese 50.
Tel 06 687 4927.
Expensive
Cuisine ranges from traditional Roman to international dishes.

Al Pompiere
Map D4. S. M. del Calderari 38.
Tel 06 686 8377.
Moderate
Excellent Roman-Jewish cuisine. Try the carciofi alla giudia (deep-fried artichokes).

Thien Kim
Map C4. Via Giulia 20.
Tel 06 6830 7832.
Cheap
Serving exquisite Vietnamese food in a tranquil ambience.

See p96 for price codes.

CAFÉS AND BARS

Caffè Farnese
Map D4. Piazza Farnese 106.
A chic, friendly spot, buzzing with the smart set sipping their wine at outside tables.

La Vineria
Map D4. Campo de' Fiori 15.
Long-standing wine bar, with open-air living rooms. Perfect for a sociable apéritif.

SHOPPING

Momento
Map D4. Piazza Cairoli 9. *The gold mine of mid-range women's fashion; from casual to elegant.*

Spazio Sette
Map D4. Via del Barbieri 7.
The best interior design products under frescoed ceilings.

QUIRINAL

Mainly a residential area in Imperial times, this original hill of Rome housed grand baths and temples. It was abandoned in the Middle Ages, but returned to favour in the late 16th century, when the prime site was claimed for the pope's new palace. Great families such as the Colonna and the Aldobrandini had their palazzi lower down the hill. With the end of papal rule in 1870, the Quirinal became the residence of the kings of Italy, then of the Italian president.

SIGHTS AT A GLANCE

Churches
Sant'Andrea al Quirinale ❸

Museums and Galleries
Museo Nazionale Romano
(Palazzo Massimo) ❺

Historic Piazzas
Piazza della Repubblica ❻

Historic Buildings
Palazzo del Quirinale ❶

Fountains and Statues
Moses Fountain ❹
Trevi Fountain ❷

SEE ALSO

• *Street Life p49.*

KEY

Ⓜ	Metro station
🛈	Tourist information

0 meters   300
0 yards   300

◀ *Fontana delle Naiadi in Piazza della Repubblica*

Palazzo del Quirinale, official residence of the president of Italy

Palazzo del Quirinale ❶

Map F3. Piazza del Quirinale. Open Sun am. Closed summer & public hols. Adm charge.

Rome's largest palace was built in 1574 as a summer papal residence, to escape the endemic malaria around the Vatican. In 1870 it became the residence of the kings of Italy and, since 1947, Italy's presidents have held official functions here.

Trevi Fountain ❷

Map E3. Fontana di Trevi.

Nicola Salvi designed Rome's largest and most famous fountain in the 18th century. Ingeniously grafted on to the back of a palazzo, the Trevi marks the end of the 19 BC Aqua Virgo aqueduct, built by Agrippa from a spring miraculously found by a virgin. The central figures are Neptune flanked by two Tritons.

Detail of Triton and "sea horse" at Rome's grandest fountain, the Trevi

Sant'Andrea al Quirinale ❸

Map F3. Via del Quirinale 29. Open daily. Closed pm in Aug.

Known as the "Pearl of the Baroque" because of its beautiful roseate marble interior, Sant'Andrea was designed by Bernini and executed by his assistants between 1658 and 1670. For such a small church, the impact is surprisingly grand, with canonical elements blended with sculptural decoration to produce an elegant harmony. Do not miss the adjacent rooms of St Stanislas Kostka.

Graceful interior of Bernini's oval Sant'Andrea al Quirinale

Moses Fountain ❹

Map G3. Fontana dell'Acqua Felice, Piazza San Bernardo.

The 16th-century structure, with three elegant arches, was designed by Domenico Fontana to mark the end of the Acqua Felice aqueduct. Offically known as Fontana dell'Acqua Felice, the fountain owes its popular name to the statue of Moses in its central niche. The side reliefs illustrate water stories from the Old Testament. The four lions are copies of Egyptian originals, now in the Vatican Museums.

Piazza della Repubblica and the Fontana delle Naiadi

Museo Nazionale Romano (Palazzo Massimo) ❺

Map G3. Palazzo Massimo, Largo di Villa Peretti 1. Open Tue–Sun. Closed 1 Jan, 1 May, 25 Dec. Adm charge is valid for the museum's five branches.

Founded in 1889, the Museo Nazionale Romano holds most of the antiquities found in Rome since 1870 as well as pre-existing collections. It is also one of the world's leading museums of Classical art. It now has five branches, of which the Palazzo Massimo houses the most impressive frescoes, mosaics and sculptures.

Piazza della Repubblica ❻

Map G3.

The piazza owes its old name, Piazza Esedra, to its shape of a semicircular recess (*exedra*). Banks, travel agencies and cafés have replaced the elegant shops that once stood under its 19th-century colonnades.

STREET LIFE

RESTAURANTS

Andrea
Map F2. Via Sardegna 28.
Tel 06 482 1891.
Expensive
Expensive menu, featuring some regal lobster dishes.

Antica Birreria Peroni
Map E4. Via di San Marcello 19. Tel 06 679 5310.
Cheap
Art Nouveau beer house serving generous portions of plain but tasty food.

Colline Emiliane
Map F3. Via degli Avignonesi 22.
Tel 06 481 7538.
Moderate
Intimate trattoria, serving up excellent meats.

See p96 for price codes.

CAFÉS

Dagnino
Map G3. Via Vittorio Emanuele Orlando 75. Tel 06 481 8660.
Rome's favourite spot for sampling Sicilian pastries.

SHOPPING

Le Gallinelle
Map F4. Via del Boschetto 76.
New and second-hand clothes, from the dramatic to the classic.

Fiorucci
Map F4. Via Nazionale 236.
Hot pink and lace from the 1980s, for fashionistas and trendy youngsters.

Spazio Artigiano
Map F4. Vicolo dei Serpenti 13.
Italian ceramics and high-quality handcrafted homeware.

ESQUILINE

In ancient times Esquiline, the largest and highest of Rome's seven hills, was largely residential, with crowded slums on its western slopes and upper-class villas on the eastern side. One of the poorer quarters of the city today, the area is heavily built up, except a small hill to the south, where lie the remains of the Baths of Titus, the Baths of Trajan and Nero's Domus Aurea. The churches, however, are the main attraction in this district steeped in history and religious mystique.

SIGHTS AT A GLANCE

Churches
San Pietro in Vincoli **1**
Santa Maria Maggiore **2**
Santa Prassede **3**

Museums
Museo Nazionale d'Arte
  Orientale **4**

Ancient Sites
Domus Aurea **5**

SEE ALSO

• *Street Life p53*

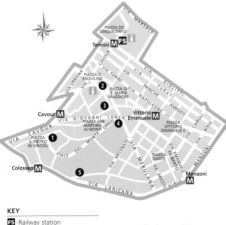

KEY

FS Railway station

M Metro station

i Tourist information

| 0 meters | 300 |
| 0 yards | 300 |

◀ *Southern façade of Santa Maria Maggiore by night*

San Pietro in Vincoli ❶

Map F4. Piazza di San Pietro in Vincoli 4a. Open daily. Free.

The original shrine was built in the 4th century to house the two chains used to shackle St Peter in prison. The chains are still here, displayed below the high altar. The church is famed for Michelangelo's Tomb of Pope Julius II, commissioned in 1505. The powerful restored statue of *Moses* was just one of the 40 the artist planned for decorating the tomb but never finished. The horns on Moses's head should really be beams of light – they are the result of the Hebrew original from the Old Testament being wrongly translated.

Moses in San Pietro

Santa Maria Maggiore ❷

Map G4. Piazza di Santa Maria Maggiore. Open daily. Free.

One of Rome's greatest basilicas, this church blends different architectural styles. Its colonnaded triple nave is part of the original 5th-century building. The Cosmatesque marble floor and Romanesque bell tower are medieval. The coffered ceiling is Renaissance, and the twin domes, front and rear façades are Baroque. The mosaics are Santa Maria Maggiore's most famous feature. From the 5th century come the biblical scenes in the nave and the superb mosaics on the triumphal arch. The basilica's medieval highlights include a 13th-century enthroned Christ in the loggia.

Apse mosaic, Santa Maria Maggiore

Santa Prassede ❸

Map G4. Via Santa Prassede 9a. Open daily. Closed Aug am. Free.

Built in the 9th century over a 2nd-century oratory, the church retains the original design, despite restorations. In the central nave, a stone slab covers the well where St Prassede reputedly buried the remains of 2,000 martyrs. Byzantine artists decorated the apse as well as the walls and vaults of the Chapel of St Zeno, with mosaics.

Museo Nazionale d'Arte Orientale ❹

Map G4. Via Merulana 248. Open Tue–Sun. Closed 1 Jan, 1 May, 25 Dec. Adm charge.

The museum's fascinating collection ranges from prehistoric Iranian ceramics, sculpture from Afghanistan, Nepal and India to Tibetan and Japanese paintings. The finds from the Italian excavation of the ancient civilization of Swat in Pakistan are of main interest.

Domus Aurea ⑤

Map G5. Viale della Domus Aurea 1. Closed for restoration.

Surviving only in parts today, this was an extravagantly opulent palace which occupied a rather large area, with a giant gilded statue of Nero who built it, and its own forest where exotic animals roamed. Excavations here have revealed large frescoes, and mosaics, thought to be a bird's-eye view of Rome.

Frescoed room in Domus Aurea

STREET LIFE

RESTAURANTS

Agata e Romeo
Map G4. Via Carlo Alberto 45.
Tel 06 446 6115.
Expensive
For serious food lovers, with an 8-course gastronomic menu.

La Gallina Blanca
Map G3. Via Antonio Rosmini 9.
Tel 06 474 3777.
Cheap
Popular for Neapolitan thick-crust pizzas.

Scoglio di Frisio
Map G4. Via Merulana 256.
Tel 06 487 2765.
Moderate
Neapolitan restaurant serving good pizza and seafood.

Sette
Map G4. Radisson SAS Hotel,
Via Filippo Turati 171. Tel 06
444 841.
Expensive
Sleek poolside dining room, attracting a glamorous crowd.

Trattoria Monti
Map G4. Via San Vito 13a.
Tel 06 446 6573.
Moderate
Excellent cuisine with a touch of the Marche region.

See p96 for price codes.

BARS

Café Bohémien
Map F4. Via degli Zingari 36.
Hub of actors, designers, with an 18th-century chandelier.

The Fiddler's Elbow
Map G4. Via dell'Olmata 43.
Rome's original Irish pub still packs in the punters.

Zest
Map G4. Radisson SAS Hotel,
Via Filippo Turati 171. *A sleek interior and superb cocktails.*

SHOPPING

LOL
Map F4. Piazza degli Zingari 11.
Unique store with unusual clothes and silver jewellery.

Nuovo Mercato Esquilino
Map G4. Via Principe Amedeo.
The biggest morning market for fresh produce.

Oviesse
Map H4. Piazza Vittorio
Emanuele 108–12. *Inexpensive clothes, plus a large selection of cosmetics and toiletries.*

Panella, L'Arte del Pane
Map G4. Via Merulana 54.
Sweets and savouries at this patisserie and bread shop.

LATERAN

In the Middle Ages the Lateran Palace was the residence of the popes, with the splendid San Giovanni beside it. After the return of the popes from Avignon at the end of the 14th century, the area declined in importance, although pilgrims still continued to visit San Giovanni and Santa Croce in Gerusalemme. When Rome became capital of Italy in 1870, a network of residential streets was laid out here for the newcomers. Archaeological interest lies chiefly in the Aurelian Wall and the ruins of the Aqueduct of Nero.

SIGHTS AT A GLANCE

Churches

San Clemente **4**
San Giovanni in Laterano **1**
Santa Croce
  in Gerusalemme **2**
Santi Quattro Coronati **3**
Santo Stefano Rotondo **5**

SEE ALSO

- Street Life p57

KEY

— City wall

M Metro station

| 0 meters | 300 |
| 0 yards | 300 |

◄ 15th-century apse fresco in Santa Croce in Gerusalemme

Cloisters in San Giovani in Laterno

San Giovanni in Laterano ❶

Map H5. Piazza di San Giovanni in Laterano 4. Cloister & baptistry open daily. Museum open Mon–Sat. Adm charge for museum & cloister.

Until 1870 all popes were crowned in Rome's first Christian basilica, built by Constantine. Rebuilt several times, it retains its original shape. Borromini undertook the last major rebuild of the interior in 1646, and the main façade is an 18th-century addition. As the Bishop of Rome, the pope celebrates Maundy Thursday mass here.

Santa Croce in Gerusalemme ❷

Map J5. Piazza di Santa Croce in Gerusalemme 12. Open daily. Free.

Built by St Helena in AD 320, this church houses the relics of the Crucifixion, including the pieces of Christ's Cross and part of Pontius Pilate's inscription hailing Jesus as the king of Jews. In the crypt is a Roman statue of Juno transformed into St Helena by replacing the head and arms and adding a cross.

Santi Quattro Coronati ❸

Map G5. Via dei Santi Quattro Coronati 20. Open daily. Free.

Named after four Christian soldiers martyred for refusing to worship a pagan god, this 4th-century AD convent was the bastion of the pope's residence, the Lateran Palace. It was rebuilt in 1084, with the delightful inner cloister added in the 13th century. The remains of medieval frescoes are housed in the Chapel of Santa Barbara, but the main attraction is the Chapel of St Sylvester with its superb frescoes depicting the legend of Constantine's conversion to Christianity.

Cloister of Santi Quattro Coronati

San Clemente ❹

Map G5. Via di San Giovanni in Laterano. Open daily. Adm to excavations.

San Clemente provides three architectural layers to unravel Rome's history. A 12th-century church lies above a 4th-century church, below which are ancient Roman buildings, including a Temple of Mithras. The upper levels are dedicated to St Clement, the fourth pope, whose life is

Statue of St Helena, Santa Croce

An apse mosaic at San Clemente

illustrated in some of the frescoes in the older church. The site was taken over in the 17th century by Irish Dominicans, who still continue the excavating work begun by Father Mullooly in 1857.

Santo Stefano Rotondo ❺

Map G6. Via di Santo Stefano Rotondo 7. Open Tue–Sun (am only Sun)

The unusual circular plan of this 5th-century church features four chapels in the shape of a cross, with four concentric corridors surrounding the inner area. Florentine architect Battista Alberti supervised the restoration in the 15th century, when an archway was added in the centre. In the 16th century the church walls were frescoed by Niccolò Pomarancio with gruesome illustrations of the martyrdom of several saints.

Distinctive circular outline of Santo Stefano Rotondo

STREET LIFE

RESTAURANTS

Charly's Saucière
Map G5. Via San Giovanni in Laterano 270.
Tel 06 7049 5666.
Expensive
Excellent Swiss-French menu accompanied by French wines.

Crab
Map G5. Via Capo d'Africa 2.
Tel 06 7720 3636.
Expensive
Simply prepared, beautifully presented seafood.

La Tana dei Golosi
Map G5. Via di San Giovanni in Laterano 220.
Tel 06 7720 3202.
Moderate
A simple spartan interior allows the authentic Italian cuisine to speak for itself.

Cannavota
Map H5. Piazza San Giovanni in Laterano 20.
Tel 06 7720 5007.
Cheap
Seafood risotto is a star attraction at this traditional neighbourhood restaurant.

BARS

Coming Out
Map G5. Via San Giovanni in Laterano 8. *Lively, unpretentious gay bar, ever bustling from late afternoon till the early hours.*

SHOPPING

Soul Food
Map G5. Via di San Giovanni in Laterano 192–4. *A good range of LPs and CDs, as well as gadgets, posters and books.*

See p96 for price codes.

NVSALVMNVS

CARACALLA

A fashionable address in Imperial Rome, the Celian Hill retains some of its vanished splendour in the vast ruins of the Baths of Caracalla. Today it is a green wedge, through which runs Via di Porta San Sebastiano, leading to one of the best-preserved gates in the ancient city wall.

SIGHTS AT A GLANCE

Churches
San Gregorio Magno ❷
Santa Maria in Domnica ❸
Santi Giovanni e Paolo ❶

Historic Buildings
Baths of Caracalla ❻

Tombs
Columbarium of
  Pomponius Hylas ❺

Parks and Gardens
Villa Celimontana ❹

SEE ALSO
• Street Life p61

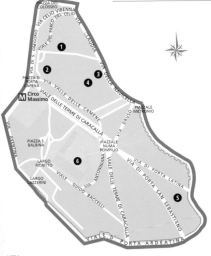

KEY
--- City wall
Ⓜ Metro station

| 0 meters | 300 |
| 0 yards | 300 |

◀ Mosaic of an athlete from the Baths of Caracalla

Nave of Santi Giovanni e Paolo

Santi Giovani e Paolo ❶

Map F5. Piazza Santi Giovanni e Paolo 13. Church open daily. Roman houses open Thu–Mon.

This church is dedicated to two 4th-century martyrs, who were beheaded here on the orders from Emperor Julian. Their remains are preserved in the chandelier-lit nave that assumed its present shape in the 18th century. However, except for the Late Baroque interior, much of the church is pure medieval in origin. The base of the bell tower was constructed from the 1st-century Temple of Claudius that once stood here.

San Gregorio Magno ❷

Map F6. Piazza di San Gregorio 1. Open daily. Free.

Named after its founder, St Gregory the Great, this 6th-century church was rebuilt in medieval times and

restored in 1629–33 by Battista Soria. The 18th-century Baroque interior was remodelled by Francesco Ferrari. Leading off the chapel of St Gregory is another small chapel, housing the saint's episcopal throne. Three small chapels stand outside, containing frescoes by Domenichino and Guido Reni.

Santa Maria in Domnica ❸

Map G6. Piazza della Navicella 12. Open daily. Free.

Dating from the 7th century, the church was made from an ancient stone galley, probably a temple offering of a Roman traveller for his safe return to the city. In the 16th century Pope Leo X added the portico and the coffered ceiling. In the apse behind the modern altar is a superb 9th-century mosaic commissioned by Pope Paschal I, who is depicted at the feet of the Virgin and Child.

Villa Celimontana ❹

Map F6. Piazza della Navicella. Park open daily. Free.

The dukes of Mattei built this formal garden in the 16th century as part of their villa. The well-kept park is now

Apse mosaic of the Virgin and Child in Santa Maria in Domnica

home to the Italian Geographical Society. It also houses ancient ruins from the family collection, including an Egyptian obelisk. It hosts an excellent jazz festival every summer.

Niches for funerary urns in the Columbarium of Pomponius Hylas

Columbarium of Pomponius Hylas ❺

Map G7. Via di Porta Latina 10. Open by appt only: permit needed. Tel 06 6710 3819.

Resembling a *columba* (dovecote), this kind of vaulted tomb was usually built by rich Romans to house the cremated remains of their freedmen. This one, excavated in 1831, dates from the 1st century AD.

An inscription mentions Pomponius Hylas and his wife. The tomb could have been a commercial venture.

Baths of Caracalla ❻

Map F6. Viale delle Terme di Caracalla 52. Open daily. Closed Mon pm, 1 Jan, 25 Dec. Adm charge.

Completed by Emperor Caracalla in AD 217, the baths functioned until AD 546, when Goths destroyed the aqueducts. A Roman bath generally featured spaces for exercise, libraries, art galleries and gardens. Most of the rich marble decorations were removed by the Farnese family in the 16th century. Today, ruins of individual rooms can be seen.

Part of one of the gymnasia in the Baths of Caracalla

STREET LIFE

RESTAURANTS

Court Delicati
Map F6. Viale Aventino 41.
Cheap
Decent Chinese restaurant with some Thai and Indonesian specialities.

Romolo e Remo
Map G6. Largo Pannonia 22–26.
Tel 06 7720 8187.
Cheap
Traditional Roman cuisine including over 40 pasta dishes.

Tramonti & Muffati
Map F6. Via di Santa Maria Ausiliatrice 105.
Tel 06 780 1342.
Moderate
Creative cooking, good wines.

BARS

Celimontana Café
Map F5. Via Claudia 14.
A large selection of beers and tasty cold dishes.

See p96 for price codes.

AVENTINE

Largely residential, yet serene, Aventine offers some unique historic sights. The top of the hill has splendid views, while at its foot ancient Rome is preserved in the two tiny Temples of the Forum Boarium and the Circus Maximus. The liveliest streets are in Testaccio, the area's social hub.

SIGHTS AT A GLANCE

Churches and Temples
San Giovanni Decollato **3**
San Saba **5**
Santa Maria della
  Consolazione **2**
Santa Maria in Cosmedin **1**
Temples of the Forum
  Boarium **4**

Ancient Sites
Circus Maximus **6**

SEE ALSO

● *Street Life p65*

KEY

— City wall

M Metro station

0 meters		300
0 yards		300

Santa Maria's fine marble mosaic floor and graceful Gothic canopy

Santa Maria in Cosmedin ❶

Map E5. Piazza della Bocca della Verità 18. Open daily. Free.

Despite its Greek epithet, *in cosmedin* (decorated), this 6th-century church is largely unadorned. Only some of the embellishment remains, such as the elegant 12th-century Romanesque bell tower and portico. Many fine examples of Cosmati work have also survived, in particular the mosaic pavement, the raised choir, and the canopy over the main altar. The main sight, however, is the Bocca della Verità, the mouth that snaps shut on the hands of liars.

Santa Maria della Consolazione ❷

Map E5. Piazza della Consolazione 94. Open daily. Free.

The church stands near the foot of the Tarpeian Rock, the site of public execution of traitors. In 1385, an accused nobleman placed an image of the Virgin Mary, to provide consolation to prisoners in their final moments. Hence the name of the church that was built here in 1470. The Early Baroque façade was added in the 16th century by Martino Longhi. The 11 side-chapels are owned by noble families and local crafts guild members. The famed image of Mary in the prebystery is attributed to Romano.

San Giovanni Decollato ❸

Map E5. Via di San Giovanni Decollato 22. Currently closed for restoration.

The main altar of the 15th-century church is dominated by Giorgio Vasari's *The Beheading of St John*, while the frescoes in the oratory depict the life of the saint. Pope Innocent VIII dedicated this site to a Florentine confraternity, whose task was to encourage condemned prisoners to repent and to give them a decent burial after they had been hanged.

Temples of Forum Boarium ❹

Map E5. Piazza della Bocca della Verità. Free.

Built in the 2nd century BC, these well-preserved temples

Tiny round Temple of Hercules

were reconsecrated as Christian churches in the Middle Ages. The rectangular temple, with Greco-Roman features, housed the image of the god of rivers and ports. Nearby is the small circular Temple of Hercules.

San Saba ❺

Map E7. Piazza G.L. Bernini 20. Open daily. Free.

Originally a 7th-century oratory for Palestinian monks fleeing from Arab invasions, the existing church is a 10th-century renovation. The portico houses a fascinating range of archaeological remains. Greek-style in floorplan, the interior decoration is mostly Cosmatesque. The greatest oddity is a 13th-century fresco showing

Detail of carving on sarcophagus in the portico of San Saba

St Nicholas, the future Santa Claus, saving three naked maidens from penury by the gift of a bag of gold.

Circus Maximus ❻

Map F6. Via del Circo Massimo. Free.

Ancient Rome's largest stadium is today little more than a long, grassy esplanade. The venue for horse and chariot races, athletic contests and wild animal fights, the Circus Maximus was continually embellished and expanded from the 4th century BC until AD 549 when the last races were held. One of its obelisks now stands in Piazza del Popolo, while the second one is in Piazza di San Giovanni in Laterano.

STREET LIFE

RESTAURANTS

L'Oasi della Birra
Map E6. Piazza Testaccio 38. Tel 06 5746 122.
Cheap
Seven-hundred beer labels and gourmet food.

Tuttifrutti
Map E6. Via Luca della Robbia 3a. Tel 06 575 7902.
Moderate
Fun, with traditional dishes.

Checchino dal 1887
Map D7. Via di Monte Testaccio 30. Tel 06 574 6318.
Expensive
Authentic Roman cuisine.

See p96 for price codes.

CAFÉS AND BARS

Akab
Map D7. Via di Monte Testaccio 69. *Plays it all, from house to R&B.*

Caffe Latino Jazz Club
Map D7. Via di Monte Testaccio 96. *Films, cabaret and disco with eclectic music.*

Caffè Emporio
Map D6. Piazza dell'Emporio 2. *Ever popular with the pre-club crowds.*

L'Alibi
Map D7. Via di Monte Testaccio 44. *Rome's famous gay disco boasts several dance floors.*

TRASTEVERE

One of the most picturesque old quarters of the city, Trastevere is inhabited by a fiercely independent people, who consider themselves the most authentic Romans. The area still holds some of its old-world charm, although the earthy, proletarian character has been threatened by the emerging fashionable restaurants, clubs and boutiques. Some of Rome's most fascinating medieval churches lie hidden away in the patchwork of narrow, cobbled backstreets, the only clue to their location an occasional glimpse of a Romanesque bell tower.

SIGHTS AT A GLANCE

Churches

San Francesco a Ripa **4**

Santa Maria in Trastevere **2**

Museums and Galleries

Sant'Egidio and Museo di Roma in Trastevere **1**

Historic Buildings

San Michele a Ripa Grande **3**

SEE ALSO

• *Street Life p69*

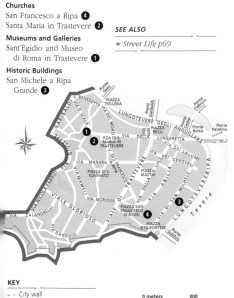

KEY

- - - City wall

ℹ️ Tourist information

| 0 meters | 300 |
| 0 yards | 300 |

◀ *A narrow alleyway between the densely packed buildings of Trastevere*

Watercolour of public scribe (1880) in the Museo di Roma in Trastevere

Sant'Egidio and Museo di Roma in Trastevere ❶

Map C5. Piazza Sant'Egidio 1. Church open Sat am. Museum open Tue–Sun.

Built in 1630, Sant'Egidio was the church of the adjoining Carmelite convent, one of many founded in the area to shelter the poor and destitute. The convent is now a museum, containing a wealth of material relating to the festivals, pastimes, superstitions and customs of the Romans when they lived under papal rule. There are old paintings and prints of the city and tableaux showing scenes of everyday life in 18th- and 19th-century Rome, including reconstructions of shops and a tavern. The museum also contains manuscripts by Rome's beloved poets Belli and Trilussa who wrote in local dialect.

Santa Maria in Trastevere ❷

Map D5. Piazza Santa Maria in Trastevere. Open daily. Free.

Probably the first official Christian place of worship to be built in Rome, this basilica became the focus of devotion to the Virgin Mary. Allegedly founded by Pope Callixtus I in the 3rd century, when Christianity was still a minority cult, the church is largely a 12th-century structure, remarkable for its mosaics. The façade mosaics are best known, mainly the one depicting Mary feeding the baby Jesus. The 22 granite columns in the nave were taken from the ruins of ancient Roman buildings.

Mosaic on the façade of Santa Maria in Trastevere

Despite some 18th-century Baroque additions, Santa Maria has retained its medieval character, and maintains strong links with the local community.

San Michele a Ripa Grande ❸

Map D6. Via di San Michele. Open for special exhibitions only.

This imposing complex, now housing the Ministry of Culture, stretches 300 m (985 ft) along the river Tiber. It was built on the initiative of Pope Innocent XII and contained a home for the elderly, a boys' reform school, a woollen mill and various chapels. Today contemporary exhibitions are often held here.

San Francesco a Ripa ❹

Map D6. Piazza San Francesco d'Assisi 88. Open daily. Free.

The former hospice of St Francis of Assisi was rebuilt by his follower, Rodolfo Anguillara. Entirely altered in the 1680s, the church is rich in sculptures. The Paluzzi-Albertoni chapel contains Bernini's breath-taking *Ecstasy of Beata Ludovica Albertoni*.

Bernini's Ecstasy of Beata Ludovica Albertoni *in San Francesco a Ripa*

STREET LIFE

RESTAURANTS

Alberto Ciarla
Map C5. Piazza San Cosimato 42a. Tel 06 581 8668.
Expensive
Rooted in classic cuisine, with legendary seafood. An exceptional range of wines.

Antica Pesa
Map C5. Via Garibaldi 18. Tel 06 580 9236.
Expensive
Historic place with a patio garden. Mediterranean cuisine and an expensive winelist.

Da Lucia
Map C5, Vicolo del Mattonato 2b. Tel 06 580 3601.
Cheap
Family trattoria in a lovely alley, serving delicious meals.

See p96 for price codes.

CAFÉS AND BARS

Bar San Calisto
Map D5. Piazza San Calisto 3–4.
Old-style bar with a buzz.

Friends Art Café
Map D5. Piazza Trilussa 34.
Slick Plexiglas-and-chrome bar.

Mr Brown
Map D5. Vicolo del Cinque 29.
Very popular British-style bar.

SHOPPING

Almost Corner Bookshop
Map D5. Via del Moro 45.
Pretty store, stocks all genres.

Enoteca Ferrara
Map D5. Via del Moro 1.
Sells top regional ingredients.

Officina della Carta
Map D5. Via Benedetta 26b.
Quaint paper workshop.

JANICULUM

Rome's traditional fortress, the Janiculum Hill defended the city for the last time in 1849, when Garibaldi held off the French troops. The park at the summit, filled with monuments to Garibaldi and his men offers great views and is popular for walks and amusements. In medieval times most of the hill was occupied by monasteries and convents. The Renaissance saw the growth of the riverside area, with opulent houses for the rich.

SIGHTS AT A GLANCE

Churches and Temples
Tempietto del Bramante **5**

Museums and Galleries
Palazzo Corsini and Galleria
  Nazionale d'Arte Antica **2**

Historic Buildings
Villa Farnesina **1**

Fountains
Fontana dell'Acqua Paola **6**

Monuments
Garibaldi Monument **4**

Parks and Gardens
Botanical Gardens **3**

SEE ALSO

• Street Life p73

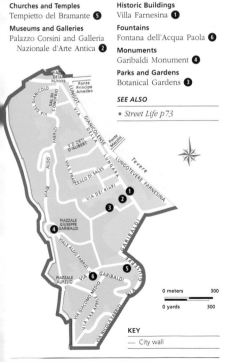

KEY

--- City wall

◀ The staircase fountain in the Botanical Gardens

Villa Farnesina ❶

Map C4. Via della Lungara 230. Open Mon–Sat. Adm charge.

Peruzzi designed this lavish 16th-century palace for a Sienese banker, Agostino Chigi, although it was bought by Alessandro Farnese in 1577. With a central block and projecting wings, it was one of the true Renaissance villas. Beautiful frescoes adorn the interiors, depicting Classical myths. Some were painted by Peruzzi himself, while the more elaborate ones were added later by Sebastiano del Piombo, Raphael and his pupils. The museum is best known for being the home of Raphael's *Triumph of Galatea*.

Raphael's Three Graces in the loggia of Cupid and Psyche, Villa Farnese

Palazzo Corsini & Galleria Nazionale d'Arte Antica ❷

Map C4. Via della Lungara 10. Open Tue–Sun. Closed 1 Jan, 1 May, 25 Dec. Adm charge.

Originally built between 1510–12 and rebuilt in the 18th century, this historic palace has hosted luminaries and been the backdrop to momentous events. Today it houses the outstanding Galleria Nazionale d'Arte Antica, also known as Galleria Corsini, featuring paintings by Rubens, Van Dyck and Fra Angelico, together with 17th- and 18th-century Italian regional art. The Accademia dei Lincei, founded in 1603, is also here.

A triptych by Fra Angelico in the Galleria Nazionale d'Arte Antica

Botanical Gardens ❸

Map C5. Largo Cristina di Svezia 24, off Via Corsini. Open Mon–Sat. Closed public hols & Aug. Adm charge.

These tranquil gardens, originally part of the Palazzo Corsini, contain more than 7,000 plant species from all over the world. Splendid collections of orchids and bromeliads, as well as indigenous and exotic species are housed here.

Garibaldi Monument ❹

Map C5. Piazzale Giuseppe Garibaldi. Free.

Erected by Emilio Gallori in 1895, this huge equestrian statue is part of a commemorative park, recalling the heroic events witnessed on the Janiculum when the French army attacked the city in 1849.

Tempietto del Bramante ➎

Map C5. Piazza San Pietro in Montorio. Open Tue–Sun. Free.

Completed in 1502, this Bramante-designed Doric rotunda is an example of early Christian *martyria*, or chapels built on the site of a saint's martyrdom. It was believed that St Peter was crucified here. The domed chapel is surrounded by 16 columns, topped by a Classical frieze and a delicate balustrade. Despite the tiny scale, Bramante's masterly use of Classical proportions creates a stunning harmony.

Fontana dell'Acqua Paola

Fontana dell'Acqua Paola ➏

Map C5. Via Garibaldi. Free.

This fountain honours the reopening in 1612 of an aqueduct built by Trajan in AD 109. The aqueduct was renamed the "Acqua Paola" after Pope Paul V, who ordered its restoration. When it was first built, the fountain had five small basins, but in 1690 Carlo Fontana altered the design, adding the huge basin you can see today. Despite many laws intended to deter them, Romans use this convenient pool of fresh water for bathing and washing their vegetables.

Bramante's round chapel, the Tempietto

STREET LIFE

RESTAURANTS

Antico Arco
Map C5. Piazzale Aurelio 7.
Tel 06 581 5274.
Expensive
Classic Mediterranean dishes, with an innovative twist.

Da Giovanni
Map C4. Via della Lungara 41a.
Tel 06 686 1514.
Cheap
Tiny trattoria that serves good, filling traditional Roman fare.

Lo Scarpone
Map C5. Via San Pancrazio 15.
Tel 06 581 4094.
Moderate
Rustic decor with a pretty garden. Fish is a speciality.

See p96 for price codes.

VATICAN

As the site where St Peter was martyred and buried, the Vatican became the residence of the popes who succeeded him. Decisions taken here have shaped the destiny of Europe, and the great basilica of St Peter's draws pilgrims from all over the Christian world. The papal palaces beside St Peter's house the Vatican Museums. With the added attractions of Michelangelo's Sistine Chapel and the Raphael Rooms, their wonderful collections of Classical sculpture make them the finest museums in Rome. The Vatican's position as a state within a state was guaranteed by the Lateran Treaty of 1929, marked by the building of a new road, the Via della Conciliazione. This leads from St Peter's to Castel Sant'Angelo, a significant historical monument.

SIGHTS AT A GLANCE

Churches and Temples
St Peter's *pp76–7* ❶

Museums and Galleries
Vatican Museums ❷

Historic Buildings
Castel Sant'Angelo ❸

SEE ALSO

• *Street Life p79*

KEY

---- City Wall

Ⓜ Metro station

ℹ Tourist information

0 meters   500

0 yards   500

◀ Dome of St Peter's dominating the Vatican skyline

St Peter's ❶

The original shrine of the epicentre of Christianity was erected on St Peter's tomb in the 2nd century. The first church, built around AD 349 by Constantine, gave way to a sumptuous basilica with Michelangelo's vast dome in the 16th century.

The dome by Michelangelo at 136 m (450 ft) is the tallest in the world. The spectacular cupola, 136 m (450 ft) high, gives unity to the majestic interior of the basilica.

The papal altar, in its present shape, dates from the reign of Clement VIII (1592–1605).

Pope Urban VIII's keys to the Kingdom of Heaven are featured on his coat of arms under the baldacchino.

Baldacchino, a magnificent 17th-century canopy of gilded bronze supported on spiral columns 20 m (66 ft) high, was designed by Bernini.

Pietà, the famous marble sculpture was finished in 1499 when Michelangelo was only 25. It stands in a chapel to one side of the nave, protected by glass since being damaged in 1972.

St Peter is shown with a filigree halo in this famed 13th-century statue, once believed to be late Roman, now attributed to Arnolfo di Cambio.

The two minor cupolas at the corners of the transept are by Vignola.

Antonio Averulino's bronze door, finished in 1445, came from the original basilica.

The nave's total length is 218 m (715 ft).

Façade by Carlo Maderno (1614)

Stairs to the dome

Entrances

Atrium of the Four Gates, Vatican Museums

Vatican Museums ➋

Map B3. Città del Vaticano. Entrance in Viale Vaticano 100. Open Mon–Fri; Sat and last Sun of each month. Closed religious hols. Special permit needed for Raphael Loggia, Vatican Library, Lapidary Gallery & Vatican Archives. Adm charge; free last Sun of month.

Four centuries of papal patronage and connoisseurship have resulted in one of the world's great collections of Classical and Renaissance art. The museum's greatest treasures are its Greek and Roman antiquities, on display since the 18th century. The 19th century saw the addition of exciting discoveries from

Etruscan tombs and excavations in Egypt. Some of the great archaeological finds of central Italy include the Laocoön group, discovered in 1506 on the Esquiline, the Apollo del Belvedere and the Etruscan bronze known as *The Mars of Todi*.

During the Renaissance, parts of the museums were decorated with wonderful frescoes commissioned for the Sistine Chapel, the Raphael Rooms and the Borgia Apartment. The walls of the Sistine Chapel were frescoed by Perugino, Ghirlandaio, Botticelli and Signorelli as well as Michelangelo, who added the great altar wall fresco, *The Last Judgement*. The ceiling fresco – the chapel's star attraction – is Michelangelo's masterpiece.

The Raphael Rooms, begun in 1508, established Raphael's reputation as an artist in Rome. The striking collection of contemporary religious art in the Borgia Apartment includes paintings by modern painters such as Klee, Munch and Braque.

Michelangelo's colourful fresco, decorating the ceiling of the Sistine Chapel

Castel Sant'Angelo ❸

Map C3. Lungotevere Castello 50 (entrance through gardens to the right of building). Piazza Cavour. Open Tue–Sun. Closed 1 Jan, 25 Dec. Adm charge.

The massive fortress of Castel Sant'Angelo takes its name from the vision that Pope Gregory the Great had of the Archangel Michael on this site. It began life in AD 139 as Emperor Hadrian's mausoleum. Since then it has had many roles: as part of Emperor Aurelian's city wall, as a medieval citadel and prison, and as the residence of the popes in times of political unrest. From the dank cells in the lower levels to the fine frescoed apartments of the

Staircase of Alexander VI cutting through the Castel Sant'Angelo

Renaissance popes, a 58-room labyrinthine museum covers all aspects of the castle's history. It also has a small collection of arms and armour from the Etruscan through to the 1900s, plus panoramic views from the battlements.

STREET LIFE

RESTAURANTS

Zen Sushi
Map C2. Via degli Scipioni 243.
Tel 06 321 3420.
Moderate
One of the best Japanese restaurants in town, serving excellent tempura.

Dal Toscano
Map B3. Via Germanico 58.
Tel 06 3972 5717.
Moderate
Exquisite meats and red wines. Wood-panelled dining room; outside tables in summer.

Il Bar Sotto il Mare
Map B2. Via Tunisi 27.
Tel 06 3972 8413.
Moderate
Famed for crustacean and shellfish antipasti. Grilled fish is as popular.

Osteria dell'Angelo
Map B2. Via G Bettolo 24–32.
Tel 06 372 9470.
Cheap
Timeless cuisine, great prices.

Veranda
Map C3. Hotel Columbus, Borgo Santo Spirito 73.
Tel 06 687 2973.
Expensive
The walls of the dining room are adorned with frescoes.

CAFÉS AND BARS

Cantina Tirolese
Map C2. Via Vitelleschi 23.
A buzzing beer house

Pellacchia
Map C2. Via Cola di Rienzo 105. *Mouthwatering ice creams in stunning flavours.*

See p96 for price codes.

VIA VENETO

An ancient suburb housing luxurious villas and gardens, Via Veneto reverted to open countryside after the Sack of Rome in the 5th century. Not until the 17th century did it recover its lost splendour, with the building of Palazzo Barberini. By 1900, Via Veneto had become a street of smart modern hotels and cafés. It featured prominently in Fellini's 1960 film *La Dolce Vita*, a scathing satire on the lives of film stars and idle rich, but since then has lost its position as the meeting place of the famous.

SIGHTS AT A GLANCE

Churches and Temples
Santa Maria della Vittoria **6**
Santa Susanna **5**

Historic Buildings
Palazzo Barberini **4**

Famous Streets
Via Veneto **1**

Fountains
Fontana del Tritone **3**
Fontana delle Api **2**

SEE ALSO

• *Street Life p83*

KEY

—— City wall

M Metro station

| 0 meters | | 200 |
| 0 yards | | 200 |

◀ *The onset of autumn in Via Veneto*

A lovely night view of Via Veneto

Via Veneto ❶

Map F2.

This lazy curve of a street is lined with exuberant *belle époque* hotels and canopied pavement cafés. Built during the redevelopment of Rome at the end of the 19th century, it had its heyday in the 1960s when its cafés were patronized by film stars. Today, the allure is limited mostly to tourists.

Fontana delle Api ❷

Map F3. Piazza Barberini.

One of Bernini's more modest works, the 17th-century fountain pays homage to Pope Urban VIII Barberini. Crab-like bees (*api*), the symbol of the Barberini family, appear to be sipping the water as it dribbles down into the basin. A Latin inscription informs us that the water is for the use of the public and their animals.

Bernini's Fontana delle Api

Fontana del Tritone ❸

Map F3. Piazza Barberini.

Bernini created this lively fountain in 1642, shortly after the completion of Pope Urban VIII Barberini's palace. Made of travertine that takes on a warm honey colour, the central figure of the sea god Triton blowing his conch shell is one of Rome's most appealing and memorable.

The Triton and his conch shell in Bernini's Fontana del Tritone

Palazzo Barberini ❹

Map F3. Via delle Quattro Fontane 13. Open Tue–Sat, except public hols. Adm charge.

Carlo Maderno designed this palace for Pope Urban VIII as a typical rural villa. When Maderno died in 1629, Bernini took over, assisted by Borromini. Of the many sumptuously decorated rooms, the most striking is the Gran Salone, with an illusionistic ceiling fresco by Pietro da Cortona. The palazzo also houses 13th–16th century paintings, part of the Galleria Nazionale d'Arte Antica.

Santa Susanna ⑤

Map F3. Via XX Settembre 15. Open daily. Free.

This Catholic church for Americans in Rome has a vigorous Baroque façade by Carlo Maderno, finished in 1603. Christians have worshipped on the site since at least the 4th century. In the nave, tapestry-like frescoes by Baldassarre Croce depict scenes from the saint's life.

Santa Maria della Vittoria ⑥

Map F3. Via XX Settembre 17. Open daily. Free.

This 17th-century Baroque church contains one of Bernini's most ambitious sculptural works, *The Ecstasy*

Bernini's The Ecstasy of St Teresa *in the Cornaro Chapel*

of St Teresa, centrepiece of the Cornaro Chapel. Built to resemble a miniature theatre, the chapel even has an audience: sculptures of the chapel's benefactor, Cardinal Federico Cornaro, and his ancestors.

STREET LIFE

RESTAURANTS

Sardegna
Map F2. Via Sardegna 34.
Tel 06 4201 6296.
Expensive
Traditional Sardinian cuisine.

Papà Baccus
Map F2. Via Toscana 36.
Tel 06 4274 2808.
Expensive
Excellent Tuscan specialities.

Mirabelle
Map F2. Via di Porta Pinciana 14. Tel 06 4216 8838.
Expensive
Memorable views and cuisine.

Taverna Flavia
Map G2. Via Flavia 9.
Tel 06 474 5214.
Moderate
Celebrated for excellent fish.

See p96 for price codes.

CAFÉS AND BARS

Cafe de Paris
Map F2. Via Veneto 90. *A magical place for an espresso.*

Gran Caffè Doney
Map F2. Via Veneto 145. *Sip coffee under the magnolias.*

Harry's Bar
Map F2. Via Veneto 150.
Clubby American style.

Jackie O'
Map F2. Boncompagni 11.
Hot watering hole and club.

SHOPPING

Brioni
Map F2. Via Veneto 12.
Elegant men's fashion.

Bruno Magli
Map F2. Via Veneto 70a.
High-end footwear store.

FURTHER AFIELD

The large parks and a handful of isolated churches outside Rome are well worth exploring. With a day to spare, you can visit the villas of Tivoli. Traditional haunts of the English aristocrats in the 18th-century, the catacombs still offer glimpses of the rapidly vanishing Campagna, the countryside around Rome. Art lovers should not miss the museum and gallery at Villa Borghese.

SIGHTS AT A GLANCE

Towns and Areas
Tivoli ⑩

Historic Roads
Via Appia Antica ⑤

Churches
San Paolo fuori le Mura ⑨
Sant'Agnese fuori
le Mura ④

Museums and Galleries
Museo e Galleria
Borghese ②
Villa Giulia ③

Ancient Sites
Hadrian's Villa ⑬

Parks and Gardens
Villa Borghese ①
Villa d'Este ⑪
Villa Gregoriana ⑫

Tombs and Catacombs
Catacombs of Domitilla ⑦
Catacombs of San Callisto/
San Sebastiano ⑥
Tomb of Cecilia Metella ⑧

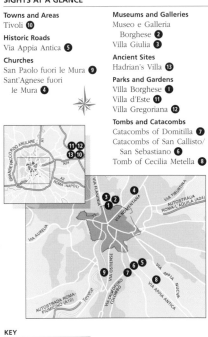

KEY

■ Main sightseeing areas

= Motorway

0 km   3

0 miles   3

◀ *Caryatids beside the canal of the Canopus at Hadrian's Villa*

Ionic temple dedicated to Aesculapius, built on the lake island

Villa Borghese ❶

Map F1. Park open daily.
Bioparco Piazzale del Giardino Zoologico 1. **Map E1.** Open daily, except 25 Dec. Adm charge.
Galleria Nazionale d'Arte Moderna Viale delle Belle Arti 131. Open Tue–Sun, except 1 Jan, 1 May, 25 Dec. Adm charge.

Designed in 1605 for Cardinal Scipione Borghese, the villa and its unique park housed garden sculpture by Bernini's father, Pietro, and dramatic waterworks built by Giovanni Fontana. The main attraction of the park lies in its long avenues lined with hedges and trees, with statues of Byron, Goethe and Victor Hugo, as well as a gloomy equestrian King Umberto I, scattered throughout. Also here are temples made to look like ruins, including the temples of Diana and Faustina, and a shrine dedicated to Aesculapius, the god of health. The on-site gallery holds a good collection of 15th–18th-century paintings.

Museo e Galleria Borghese ❷

Map F1. Villa Borghese, Piazzale Scipione Borghese 5. Open Tue–Sun, except 1 Jan, 7 Jan, 25 Dec. Advance booking recommended weekdays and obligatory Sat & Sun. Adm charge.

Cardinal Scipione was an extravagant patron of the arts and he commissioned sculptures from the young Bernini which now rank among his most famous works, such as *David*, *The Rape of Proserpine* and *Apollo and Daphne*. Today the villa houses the superb private Borghese collection of sculptures and paintings in the fabulous Museo e Galleria Borghese.

Bernini's Apollo and Daphne

Villa Giulia ❸

Map E1. Piazzale di Villa Giulia 9. Open Tue–Sun, except 1 Jan, 1 May, 25 Dec. Adm charge. Concerts in the courtyard in July.

Built as a country retreat for Pope Julius III, the villa once housed an impressive collection of statues. The villa, gardens, pavilions and fountains were designed by some of the exceptional architects of the time: Vignola, Vasari and the sculptor Ammannati. Michelangelo also contributed. Its main features are

A 4th-century BC bronze marriage coffer

4

Central Rome

Most of the sights given in this book lie within the old city wall in 16 areas shown in the map below. Each area has its own chapter. Those on a short visit may have to choose just a few central areas: the Forum, the Capitol, Piazza della Rotonda, Piazza Navona, Campo de' Fiori, Piazza di Spagna and the Vatican.

Laocoön and His Sons
This 1st-century AD marble group is housed in the Vatican Museums (see p78).

Neptune Fountain, Piazza Navona
At the north end of Piazza Navona, the basin of the Fontana di Nettuno was built by Giacomo della Porta in 1576. The statues of Neptune and the Nereids were added in the 19th century (see p32).

Piazza del Campidoglio at night

CONTENTS

INTRODUCING ROME

Main altar of Santa Maria in Campitelli

its façade, the courtyard and garden and the nymphaeum. Since 1889 Villa Giulia has housed the Museo Nazionale Etrusco, with its pre-Roman antiquities from central Italy.

Sant'Agnese fuori le Mura ❹

Via Nomentana 349. Open daily. Closed Sun am. Adm charge to catacombs.

The church stands among a group of early Christian buildings including the ruins of a covered cemetery, catacombs and the crypt where the 13-year-old martyr St Agnes was buried in AD 304. Though altered over the centuries, much of the basilica's structure remains intact. In the 7th-century apse mosaic, St Agnes appears as a Byzantine empress.

St Agnes flanked by two popes, apse mosaic in Sant'Agnese

Via Appia Antica ❺

The first part of the Via Appia, or "the Queen of Roads", was built in 312 BC by Appius Claudius. The most pastoral part begins at the Tomb of Cecilia Metella, which was made into a fortification in the Middle Ages. It leads to more tombs as well as grazing sheep and

Cypresses lining part of the Roman Via Appia Antica

the private gates to fabulous modern-day villas.

Catacombs of San Callisto/ San Sebastiano ❻

Via Appia Antica 126. Open Thu–Tue, except 1 Jan, Feb, Easter Sun, 25 Dec. Adm charge. **San Sebastiano** Via Appia Antica 136. Open Mon–Sat, except 1 Jan, Easter Sun, mid-Nov–mid-Dec, 25 Dec. Adm charge.

The early Christians buried their dead in underground cemeteries in accordance with the laws of the time. Some rooms at the vast Catacombs of San Callisto are adorned with stucco and frescoes. Many of the mausoleums at San Sebastiano are also frescoed.

Catacombs of Domitilla ❼

Via delle Sette Chiese 282. Open Wed–Mon except Jan, Easter Sun, 25 Dec. Adm charge.

This is the largest network of catacombs in Rome. Many of the tombs from the 1st and 2nd centuries AD have no Christian connection. In the burial chambers there are frescoes of both Classical and Christian scenes.

Tomb of Cecilia Metella ❽

Via Appia Antica 161. Open Tue–Sun. Adm charge.

Built for Cecilia Metella, a little-known noblewoman, this drum-shaped tomb retains some of its marble relief. It was donated in 1302 by Pope Boniface VIII to his family, who incorporated it in a fortified castle that allowed them to control the traffic on the road and exact high tolls.

19th-century mosaic on façade of San Paolo fuori le Mura

Fragments of marble relief on the Tomb of Cecilia Metella

San Paolo fuori le Mura ❾

Via Ostiense 190. Open daily. Free.

Today's church is a faithful reconstruction of the great basilica destroyed by fire in 1823. Built by Constantine in the 4th century over the spot where St Paul was buried, it was rebuilt and fortified following the sack by the Saracens in AD 846.

Tivoli ❿

31 km (20 miles) NE of Rome.

A charming hill town, with world-famous gardens and the villa of Cardinal d'Este, Tivoli has been a popular summer resort since the days of the Roman Republic. Many celebrated Romans owned villas here. With clean air and a beautiful situation on the slopes of the Tiburtini hills, it is endowed with healthy sulphur springs and the waterfalls of the Aniene. After the town suffered heavy bombing damage in 1944, its main buildings and chuches were speedily restored. The lovely cobbled streets are still lined with medieval houses.

Tivoli, a favourite place to escape the heat of the Roman summer

Villa d'Este ⓫

Piazza Trento 1, Tivoli. Open Tue–Sun, except 1 Jan, 25 Dec. Adm charge.

Cardinal Ippolito d'Este developed this 16th-century estate on the site of an old Benedictine convent. The villa's fame rests mainly on the terraced gardens and fountains laid out by Ligorio and Giacomo della Porta. The gardens have suffered neglect in the past, but the grottoes and fountains still give a vivid impression of the luxury which the princes of the church enjoyed. The main highlight is the Viale delle Cento Fontane, 100 fountains in interesting shapes such as grotesques, obelisks, eagles and ships.

The extensively restored Canopus, with replicas of the original caryatids

Hadrian's Villa ⓭

Villa Adriana, Via Tiburtina. Open daily, except 1 Jan, 1 May, 25 Dec. Adm charge.

Built as a private summer retreat between AD 118 and 134, Hadrian's Villa was a vast open-air museum of full-scale reproductions of the emperor's favourite buildings from Greece and Egypt. Although excavations on this site began in the 16th century, there are several signposted ruins, lying unidentified in the surrounding fields. One of the most impressive is the Maritime Theatre, a round pool with an island in the middle, surrounded by columns. The most ambitious of Hadrian's replicas was the Canopus, a sanctuary of the god Serapis near Alexandria. Egyptian statues decorated the temple and its grounds.

Terrace of 100 Fountains in the gardens of Villa d'Este

Villa Gregoriana ⓬

Largo Massimo, Tivoli. Open Tue–Sun. Closed Dec–Feb.

The main highlights of this steeply sloping park, named after Pope Gregory XVI, are the waterfalls and grottoes created over the centuries by the River Aniene.

Getting Around

Rome's compact old centre can be best enjoyed on foot. Driving or cycling on the bustling main streets isn't a good option, though bike or scooter rides can be great fun. Explore the city area by area, using public transport when distances are too far.

Walking

Directions for walkers

The historic centre is largely pedestrianized, but many streets are narrow, clogged with traffic and lack pavements. The cobblestones are hard on your feet, so wear sturdy shoes. Walk on the shady side of the street in summer.

Driving

Driving in central Rome is not always a very pleasant experience. Italian drivers are notorious for their recklessness, while the pedestrians step out onto the roads without warning. The one-way system operating in much of the centre makes it worse. Don't drive unless you are accustomed to driving in Italian cities. Take extra care if driving late at night: inebriated driving is not uncommon in Italy.

No stopping *No parking*

One-way street

Buses and Trams

Rome's ATAC bus network has central hubs at Termini, Piazza Venezia, Largo Argentina and Piazza San Silvestro. Newsagents sell maps; *fermata* (bus stop) signs list the routes that stop there. Buy tickets at newsstands, tobacconists or machines at major stops. Stamp the ticket on the bus: 75-minute, one-day, three-day and weekly tickets are available with unlimited transfers.

A Rome ATAC bus

Metropolitana

Not always useful to visitors, the A and B lines intersect at Termini, mainly serving the suburbs. Good tourist stops include the Spanish Steps, Colosseum, San Paolo (basilica), Ottaviano (six blocks from St Peter's), and Barberini (a few blocks from the Trevi Fountain). It uses the same tickets as buses. The "C" line, under construction, is supposed to be finished by 2014.

Phrase Book

In Emergency

Help!	**Aiuto!**	eye-**yoo**-toh
Stop!	**Fermate!**	fair-**mah**-teh
Call a doctor.	**Chiama un medico**	kee-**ah**-mah oon **meh**-dee-koh
Call an ambulance.	**Chiama un' ambulanza**	kee-**ah**-mah oon am-boo-**lan**-tsa
Call the police.	**Chiama la polizia**	kee-**ah**-mah lah pol-ee-**tsee**-ah
Call the fire brigade.	**Chiama i pompieri**	kee-**ah**-mah ee pom-pee-**air**-ee
Where is the telephone?	**Dov'è il telefono?**	dov-**eh** eel teh-**leh**-foh-noh?
The nearest hospital?	**L'ospedale più vicino?**	loss-peh-**dah**-leh pee- oo-vee-**chee**-noh?

Communication Essentials

Yes/No	**Sì/No**	see/noh
Please	**Per favore**	pair fah-**vor**-eh
Thank you	**Grazie**	**grah**-tsee-eh
Excuse me	**Mi scusi**	mee **skoo**-zee
Hello	**Buon giorno**	bwon **jor**-noh
Good bye	**Arrivederci**	ah-ree-veh-**dair**-chee
here/there	**qui/là**	kwee/lah
What?	**Quale?**	**kwah**-leh?
When?	**Quando?**	**kwan**-doh?
Why?	**Perchè?**	pair-**keh**?
Where?	**Dove?**	**doh**-veh

Useful Phrases

How are you?	**Come sta?**	**koh**-meh stah?
Very well, thank you.	**Molto bene, grazie.**	**moll**-toh **beh**-neh **grah**-tsee-eh
That's fine.	**Va bene.**	va **beh**-neh
Where is/are ...?	**Dov'è/Dove sono ...?**	dov-**eh**/doveh **soh**-noh?
Do you speak English?	**Parla inglese?**	**par**-lah een **gleh** zeh?
I don't understand.	**Non capisco.**	non ka-**pee**-skoh
Could you speak more slowly, please?	**Può parlare più lentamente, per favore?**	pwoh par-**lah**-reh pee-**oo** len-ta-**men**-teh pair fah-vor-eh?

Useful Words

big	**grande**	**gran**-deh
small	**piccolo**	**pee**-koh-loh
hot	**caldo**	**kal**-doh
cold	**freddo**	fred-doh
open	**aperto**	ah-**pair**-toh
closed	**chiuso**	kee-oo-zoh
left	**a sinistra**	ah see-**nee**-strah
right	**a destra**	ah **dess**-trah
straight on	**sempre dritto**	**sem**-preh **dree**-toh
entrance	**entrata**	en-**trah**-tah
exit	**uscita**	oo-**shee**-ta
toilet	**il gabinetto**	eel gah-bee-**net**-toh

A Vespa scooter and helmet

Bike and Moped Hire

Roman traffic makes scootering dangerous, although bikes are a great way to get around the city centre. Sundays are calmest and several roads close to traffic for bikers. Rental outfits include Roma in Scooter and Treno e Scooter. Motor-cyclists have to wear helmets by law.

Car Hire

Cars are useless in Rome itself: traffic is bad, and parking expensive and rare. If you are on a longer trip, pick up the car on your last day in Rome. Local outfits are rarely cheaper than international ones. Most companies require theft protection; check if your credit card covers this insurance.

Car hire office at Flumicino airport

Taxis

Official taxis in Rome are white and must bear the "taxi" sign on the roof. Taxi ranks are found at the airports, train stations, major squares and tourist sights. The base rate is €2, plus 50 cents per kilometre in 1-cent increments. Extra fees are charged for luggage, from 10pm to 7am, on Sundays and airport runs. It is not necessary to tip the driver.

Horse-drawn carriages

Horse-drawn Carriages

Horse drawn *caleches*, carrying up to five people, can be hired from many points, for a gentle tour of the historic centre. They can be expensive, though prices for longer rides are negotiable. Establish the price before you set off.

River Transport

Battelli di Roma runs from two embarkation points, near the Tiber Island and Castel Sant' Angelo, to Ponte Risorgimento, every half hour from 10am to 6pm.

TRAVEL INFORMATION

For bikes and mopeds: Tel 06 488 5485 (Scooters for Rent); 06 4890 5823 (Treno e Scooter). For river transport: Tel 06 9774 5498. www.battelli diroma.it For taxis: Tel 06 06 09. For Avis car hire: Tel 199 100 133. For car breakdown services: Tel 803 116.

Survival Guide

Money services are not very prompt in Rome, usually involving a lot of paperwork. The telephone system, however, has undergone a major overhaul, following deregulation. Personal security and health are also largely favourable for visitors.

MONEY

Currency
In 2002, Italy adopted the euro to replace the lira. Euro coins come in 1, 2, 5, 10, 20 and 50 euro cents and 1 and 2 euros. Notes come in €5, €10, €20, €50, €100, €200 and €500 denominations.

Credit Cards
MasterCard and Visa are accepted everywhere except the smallest shops, restaurants or hotels. American Express is also accepted in many places. Diner's Club tends to be valid only at pricier places.

Exchange office at an Italian bank

Changing Money
If you do not use an ATM, change money at a bank for the best rates, or at main post offices. Bring your passport as ID.

Traveller's Cheques
Carry a few cheques for emergencies. Buy them in dollars, pound sterling or euros. Avoid exchanging them at a shop or hotel.

Postbox with slots each for letters to Rome and other destinations

COMMUNICATIONS

Sending Letters
Italy's post can be slow – letters might arrive home in three days or three months. Any tobacconist or newsagent can supply stamps for the country to which you are mailing. Drop your mail in the slot of the postbox labelled *per tutte le altre destinazioni*.

Receiving Mail
Mail addressed to you at "FERMO POSTA/ Piazza San Silvestro 19/ 00187 Roma, Italia/ ITALY" will make it to the main post office. There's a small fee to pick it up.

Telecom Italia card telephone

Telephones

Most payphones in Italy now accept only pre-paid phonecards, which you can buy in several denominations at newsstands and tobacconists. Break off the corner before use.

Internet

Internet parlours and cafés are popping up constantly (check at the tourist office; they tend to appear and disappear frequently). Increasingly, hotels are installing a common-use computer with web access.

FARMACIA

Pharmacy sign

HEALTH AND SAFETY

Police

There are two main police branches you might deal with, the regular *polizia* and the more military-trained, national *carabinieri* force. A police station is called a *questura*.

Insurance

Check your personal insurance to see if it covers you abroad. Usually you must pay any hospital charges up front and file for reimbursement when you get

Police officer in traffic uniform

home, although Blue Cross/Blue Shield members can visit affiliated hospitals in Rome, using their card as they do at home.

Hospitals

Roman hospitals (*ospedale*) are efficient and semi-privatized. The emergency room is called *pronto soccorso*. For uncomplicated visits not requiring hospital admission, they'll usually give you a check-up, write a prescription if necessary and send you off with a smile, with no paperwork involved.

Lost Property

For items lost on a bus or Metro, contact the numbers below. Otherwise, ask at a police station. To make an insurance claim, report your loss to a police station and get a signed form. For lost passports, contact your embassy or consulate; for lost traveller's cheques, the issuing company's office. Lost property (buses, trams): Tel 06 676 93214. Lost property (metro): Tel 06 487 4309 (A line); 06 5753 2265 (B line).

EMERGENCY NUMBERS

Ambulance
· 118
(Free from any telephone)

Fire
· 115
(Free from any telephone)

Police
· 112 (*Carabinieri*)
· 113 (*Polizia*)
(Free from any telephone)

Index